Sagebrush
and
Cappuccino

Sagebrush and Cappuccino

• • • • • •

Confessions of an LA Naturalist

David Wicinas

Sierra Club Books

SAN FRANCISCO

for Pamela

The Sierra Club, founded in 1892 by John Muir, has
devoted itself to the study and protection of the earth's scenic and
ecological resources—mountains, wetlands, woodlands, wild shores and
rivers, deserts and plains. The publishing program of the Sierra Club offers books
to the public as a nonprofit educational service in the hope that they may enlarge
the public's understanding of the Club's basic concerns. The point of view
expressed in each book, however, does not necessarily represent that of
the Club. The Sierra Club has some sixty chapters coast to coast,
in Canada, Hawaii, and Alaska. For information about how you
may participate in its programs to preserve wilderness and
the quality of life, please address inquiries to Sierra Club,
730 Polk Street, San Francisco, CA 94109.

Library of Congress Cataloging-in-Publication Data

Wicinas, David.
    Sagebrush and cappuccino : confessions of an L.A. naturalist / David Wicinas.
        p.   cm.
    ISBN 0-87156-435-1 (pbk.)
        1. Natural history—California—Los Angeles Region.   2. Nature
conservation—California—Los Angeles Region.   I. Title.
QH105.C2W48   1995
508.794'94—dc20   95-4280

Production by Janet Vail
Cover design by Sharon Smith
Book design by Sandy Drooker
Composition by Wilsted & Taylor

Cover artwork by David Hockney, "Pearblossom Hwy., 11–18th April 1986"
(Detail), Second Version Photographic Collage, 78 × 111" © David Hockney

"Sepulveda TresPass" and "Face the Wind"
were previously published in the *Los Angeles Reader.*

The author gratefully acknowledges permission to quote from *Of Wolves and Men,*
by Barry Lopez. Copyright © 1978 by Barry Holstun Lopez.

Printed in the United States of America on acid-free paper containing
a minimum of 50% recovered waste paper, of which at least
10% of the fiber content is post-consumer waste
            10   9   8   7   6   5   4   3   2   1

Contents

· · · · · ·

Preface

. . . . . .

Friends tell me I have a split personality; a forest ranger trapped within me constantly struggles for control against a café-hopping *boulevardier.* I can never decide which is more important: the jolt of a strong cappuccino or the smell of wet sagebrush on a misty morning.

God knows how I wound up this way. Maybe I read too much Hemingway at an impressionable age. By the time I'd memorized *The Sun Also Rises,* I knew a man should perform with equal grace in a trout stream or a *tapas* bar. As a boy I'd waded through a few babbling brooks, but before I turned twenty years old I never set eyes on an art gallery, an opera, a good bottle of wine, or even a sidewalk café. The cultivation of my personal palate, however, is not the subject of this book. Rather, it's about reconciling those uptown urges with the other side of Hemingway's equation—the instinct to flee the city as fast as possible.

I was not raised in the north woods, on a ranch, in a swamp, or even on a farm. I was born the son of a steelworker in a blue-collar suburb of Pittsburgh, Pennsylvania. When I was young, my father often took me fishing and camping. Displaying no great love of the outdoors himself, he mainly seemed to like this type of vacation because it was cheap.

Those few weeks we spent each year in the state parks of Pennsylvania, New York, and Michigan were enough, however, to instill in me a deep reverence for nature.

By the time I reached adulthood I fancied myself a writer. (Again, blame it on Hemingway.) This delusion afflicts many young people. With me, however, the disabling symptoms did not pass. When I was twenty-eight, I emigrated to Los Angeles because I'd heard that in Hollywood writers found money and fame. I was either extremely gullible or hopelessly romantic. Or both. At least I wasn't alone. Millions of other fortune-seekers had already paved the path that leads to the Golden State.

The little forest ranger within me expressed great misgivings about Los Angeles. He'd been there; he knew. It was too urban; there were too many cars, too many people; it was too hot, too dry, and there weren't enough trees. He urged me instead to find a nice job as a forest fire lookout. But the cappuccino drinker craved the carnival of life. He won that round. I packed up my Datsun and drove west.

My misgivings about Los Angeles proved to be well-founded. Just as I had remembered, Southern California blasts the senses with an endless sea of stucco garden apartments and sun-baked six-lane boulevards that stretch for seventy-five miles in every direction. There are most definitely too many people and *way* too many cars.

Unfortunately, before I moved I did not have similar premonitions about Hollywood. I don't mean the city of Hollywood—that gritty pastiche of faded Art Deco dreams and crowded immigrant housing—but rather the fantasy that the *word* Hollywood symbolizes for the rest of the world.

Writers in Los Angeles share a maxim: "You can die here of encouragement." In my career as a Hollywood writer I achieved some quick (but minor) successes, convincing me that my personal Mother Lode was one deal away. If I just worked a little harder, eked out a little more inspiration, delivered something a little more commercial, in no time I'd be buying my tuxedo for the Oscars.

My hopes were not completely unfounded. Many of the producers I met gushed over me. Eventually I realized that in Hollywood no one ever says anything negative. Almost everyone in The Industry is so unsure of themselves, so fearful they may somehow wind up working next year for *you,* they will never make any statement that could possibly offend anyone. All opinions take the form of superlatives. You have to judge your own merit on gradations of lavish praise.

"I loved it" means no thanks and have a nice life.

"I am prostrate before your talent" means maybe you wrote something pretty good and if you're lucky they'll take your next call.

"Here's the deal memo" means you can start shopping for a new car.

Mastering the folkways of a culture is hard for any newcomer, and a society as peculiar as Hollywood poses many added difficulties. But I tried. I cranked out screenplays, plays, and articles, and all the while worked a day job. Who had time to discover what lay beyond the asphalt grid? I was too busy dying of encouragement.

After six years of feigning admiration for ineffectual twerps wearing Armani jackets, I resolved to get the monkey off my back. I was tired of postponing the life experiences that seem to satisfy everyone else in the world. Unfortunately, there is no Screenwriters Anonymous—no twelve-step program to creative and psychic independence. Recovering screenwriters face a long, painful process convincing themselves that they won't be picking up their Oscar passes.

For me, one happy benefit of deciding to lead a "normal

life" was that I finally raised my eyes to the horizons of Los Angeles.

And there on the fringes of the nation's second-largest metropolitan region—a vast city that mercilessly conglomerates millions of people—I discovered pockets of wild country. They were not hard to find. Often they lay right on the edge of the city, if not in its very heart.

The mountains and seas that surround Los Angeles poke their toes into many neighborhoods, and on any day they are apt to toss up small wonders; you're quite likely to see deer, coyotes, bobcats, hawks, dolphins, whales. If you're incredibly lucky you might see a California condor, or even a California gnatcatcher. Mountain lions prowl the same neighborhoods as movie stars. At the back door of swanky Bel Air lies a valley almost as pristine as the day Gaspar de Portolá, the first European explorer of California, walked by in 1769.

I started exploring, and the discoveries I made knocked down some mental walls I had unconsciously erected around the tight orbit of my urban life. That psychic wrecking ball revealed a broader, greener world beyond—to my great delight. But, as many Californians like to tell you, there's a yin for every yang. Every pleasure must be counterbalanced by a matching pain. To find LA's last few unspoiled spots, as I did, you must avert your eyes from the graffiti, the smog, the junked cars, the ubiquitous offal of twentieth-century civilization (to use the term loosely). If and when you do find a personal oasis, you probably should not grow too attached to it because at this very moment bulldozers may be grinding toward your little green temple.

My explorations evolved into adventures. Before I took a walk I learned everything I could about my destination. I examined not just the city's geographic frontiers but also its historical horizons. I discovered that LA boasts a rich and unique past, one shaped by dreamers and charlatans, explorers and exploiters. It is a land where for two hundred years ego-gratification has been practiced on a colossal scale. Franciscan fathers subjugated the natives and cleared the way for Spanish dons, who yielded to American adventurers, who paved the way for citrus farmers, who unlocked fortunes for real estate barons, who ushered in the oil wildcatters, who gave way to movie moguls, who invented the life of the surfer dude. Los Angeles is a geography of dreams.

The city has an equally rich natural history. As in any arid climate, life here is spare and subtle. LA's chaparral-covered hills and cloistered woodlands do not offer up the warm bath of life you might see in a meadow on a summer day in Pennsylvania. No, Southern California is landscape of basins and freshly carved mountains, carpeted with tenacious plantlife that regularly shrugs off total incineration. Muted pastels color the hills. Crystalline sunshine divides the world into harsh glare and cool, deep shadow.

It's a landscape most people must learn to appreciate. But once you have seen the hills dusted with a snowfall of wildflower blossoms, or rested at the foot of a gnarled live oak, you may well become infatuated.

The wild lands hidden on the periphery of Los Angeles are, of course, besieged. If one business has shaped Los Angeles more than movie-making, it's real estate. Fundamentally, they're two sides of the same coin—both sell dreams.

Bob Hope became one of the country's richest men not just by clowning around with Bing Crosby. He took his movie money and followed this investment rule: Go to where the houses stop and buy land. He knew the city would catch up with him. When it did, people started measuring Hope's net worth in nine figures—all to the left of the decimal point.

Plenty of developers still follow Hope's rule. Unfortunately, a young family's dream of country living far from the smog doesn't square well with California oaks. They don't thrive near asphalt. Few species do, except perhaps human beings—and pigeons.

•

As I excavated LA's wilderness gems, I discovered that by trying to learn every detail about a place and then experiencing its intimate secrets—personally—on foot—I formed a bond to a blank spot on a map.

My walks also opened a door to writing that I had locked when I forsook Hollywood. I started recounting my explorations and discovered I was enjoying myself. I delighted in the wordplay, the mental excursions, the chance to teach—and preach. But most of all, I relished the opportunity to just plain think. Exercising my legs yielded the unexpected benefit of also stretching my mind.

Perhaps the walks described in this book will inspire you to launch your own explorations—mental or physical. Discovering a few special spots, and the eyes you need to see them, might help refresh your soul, especially if it is feeling a little withered from living in the city. Possibly a sense of communion will flourish between you and a particular brook, or bird, or tree. Your journeys may convince you that even a twenty-first-century urban jungle can hold wild land worth protecting—and nurturing.

Wonders can be found everywhere. You just have to open your eyes, and your mind. With the right outlook, you can, as the poet William Blake wrote, "see a world in a grain of sand / and a heaven in a wild flower."

And if you do your exploring in a place like Los Angeles, on your way home you'll pass plenty of bustling cafés where you can order a steaming cup of cappuccino.

Sepulveda TresPass

. . . . . .

I live in Los Angeles.

Like it or not, I have fifteen million neighbors.

In a city this vast, it's easy to feel completely detached from the natural world. During an average day, the only birds we Angelenos see are pigeons, the only trees are palms. We can drive in a straight line for seventy-five miles and never be more than a few blocks from a mini-mall. Although mountains surround the city, most of us here in LA view those hills not as a destination but more as a backdrop to the theater of urban life. We are too busy chasing our dreams, or running from our fears, to walk up a dusty path into the chaparral.

Unlike many of my neighbors, however, I take a small dose of nature every day. I administer it in the Los Angeles style—from my car—while I cross Sepulveda Pass on the San Diego Freeway. Climbing more than a thousand feet at its summit, Sepulveda Pass bisects the Santa Monica Mountains, a range of rugged hills that separates the densely populated center of Los Angeles from the slightly less dense San Fernando Valley. Although humans inhabit portions of the Santa Monica Mountains, large expanses of these hills survive undeveloped, forming islands of wildness situated smack in the middle of America's second-largest city.

Every day as I drive Sepulveda Pass, making my six-mile cut through the Santa Monica Mountains, hawks soar in the morning sun and deer graze on the hillsides at twilight. On spring nights the dreamy fragrance of night-blooming jasmine blankets the canyon. During those few minutes spent in the hills, my heart lifts.

One day bulldozers appeared on a mountainside above Sepulveda Pass. Over the next weeks the earthmovers stripped away the sagebrush covering the hills, and then they blasted away a large part of the hill beneath. The bulldozers moved so much dirt, at first I mistook this activity for strip mining. Eventually they scraped out a new contour for the mountain, one that better accommodates the multimillion-dollar homes being built there today. And now I'm watching another project, the Getty Center, a much-heralded art complex, transform the undeveloped western face of the pass into a cityscape of roads, buildings, and parking garages.

Before the natural environment of Sepulveda Canyon— this expanse of land that daily lifts my spirits—is completely eradicated, I feel I should determine what I am losing. This will require some investigative work, mostly trips to the library to educate myself about the human and natural forces at play in the pass. But it will also force me to commit that most drastic of acts in Los Angeles—I will leave behind my car. I have decided to cross Sepulveda Pass on foot.

•

Sepulveda Pass has a long history of causing grief for travelers. The first European explorer of California—or Alta California as it was known then, to distinguish it from Baja California—was the Spaniard Gaspar de Portolá. On August 5, 1769, he became the first white man to commute through the pass. The route he followed was already an established

Indian trail. Miguel Constanzo, an engineer accompanying de Portolá, wrote in his diary that in the rugged mountains their pack animals were "easily frightened. The sight of a coyote or fox is sufficient to stampede them . . . and make them run many leagues, throwing themselves over precipices and cliffs."

For 160 years crossing Sepulveda Pass remained a difficult undertaking. But in the 1920s a road was built through the pass to connect the heart of the city in the Los Angeles basin to the housing developments mushrooming in the San Fernando Valley—the vast suburban community known today as simply "the Valley." Still, for many Angelenos this serpentine route was no less perilous than the trail used by Costanzo and de Portolá. Over the next three decades hundreds of people were killed in traffic accidents on winding Sepulveda Boulevard, many of them on a bend known as "dead man's curve" just south of the crest of the hill.

That malicious curve was straightened when the San Diego Freeway (Interstate 405) replaced Sepulveda Boulevard as the major artery through the pass, but driving conditions didn't improve. On the day of the freeway's opening, December 21, 1962, motorists encountered an evil portent. So many drivers lined up at the southern end of the freeway, all eager to motor its graceful curves, a SigAlert was issued *before the freeway even opened.*

(For those unaccustomed to the folkways of Southern California, I must explain that "SigAlert" is the most feared word in the lexicon of the Los Angeles commuter.* The California Department of Transportation issues SigAlerts to warn motorists about traffic obstacles of the utmost severity. If you get

---

* The SigAlert is named after a local radio station manager, Lloyd Sigmon, who in the 1950s devised a system for alerting drivers to long traffic delays. The term was recently added to the *Oxford English Dictionary*.

caught in a SigAlert, you may as well put your car in park, get out, and say hello to your neighbors. You won't be going home anytime soon.)

Back in 1962 Ed T. Telford, chief engineer at what was then called the Division of Highways, predicted the San Diego Freeway "can take 200,000 vehicles daily if traffic is spread out." Today *300,000* frazzled motorists, including myself, shoehorn our cars through the pass every single day. Strangling in traffic in the Santa Monica Mountains has one bright side: you go mad in beautiful surroundings.

•

I begin my journey from the basin to the Valley early one morning in October while a stiff Santa Ana wind kicks up. A brick-colored smudge hangs over the ocean behind me as I drive to my wilderness jump-off point, a high-tone supermarket called the Bel Air Marketplace. Ahead, the Santa Monica Mountains beckon. Their bony ridges catch the glow of the low eastern sun and cast shadows over the folded, craggy land.

Cutting the umbilical to my car, I slam the door and start walking—yes, *walking*—up Casiano Drive, a residential street in Bel Air, LA's swankiest neighborhood. The road winds up a ridge that forms the eastern face of Sepulveda Canyon. At this hour the ridge shades Casiano Drive, and that shadow gives an extra bite to the winds blasting in from the north. A block away, the traffic on the 405 rushes along, sounding like surf—minus any rhythm or romance.

As I walk, I notice in every driveway a Halloween pumpkin with some kind of sticker attached to it. I stop to inspect. The sticker says, "Compliments of Mike Glickman Realty." Where I grew up any self-respecting adolescent (if that isn't an oxymoron) would have had a field day with these pumpkins,

splattering pulp everywhere. But I suppose life is more gen-
teel in Bel Air.

Casiano Drive climbs steeply and soon I'm panting. I want
to double-time it through this residential zone before some
Bel Aryan stops me and decides I look suspicious and should
be arrested for the crime of using my feet as a means of con-
veyance. A guy in jogging shorts heads my way. Deciding
offense is the best defense, I stare directly at him, trying to
force out a good morning. Finally he yields a mumbled hello.

Passing the last house on Casiano, I step around a gate at
the end of a fire road. The Santa Monica Mountains stretch
out before me, wild and inviting. For a minute I hug the hillside to gain some shelter from the cold wind. With nothing
buffeting my ears, the soothing sound of chirping crickets
washes over me. That's a noise I don't hear for years at a time,
living in LA.

The dirt fire road parallels the 405's ten-lane torrent, two
hundred feet below. The cut for the road has exposed the rock
beneath, a wall of wildly twisting stratifications. Geologists
say that most of the rock in the Santa Monica Mountains is
metamorphic, a sedimentary shale heated up 120 million
years ago by molten rock below. Judging from that topsy-
turvy rock face, 120 million years ago was a wild time.

Recently, only one or two million years ago, elephants
roamed these hills. I see no stray pachyderms today. In fact, I
see no wildlife at all, although ground squirrel, opossum, raccoon, skunk, coyote, and mule deer thrive here. Even a few
mountain lions still prowl the more unspoiled reaches of the
Santa Monica Mountains.

Vegetation here combines chaparral and coastal sage scrub
with occasional islands of oak and sycamore. I see lots of Our
Lord's candle, a type of yucca. In the late spring this plant's

creamy flowers dot the hillsides, rising above the brush on tu-
bular stalks. I also spot a couple of toyon bushes, loaded with
orange-red berries. A century ago Angelenos mistook toyon
growing on the distant hillsides for holly. So they named these
hills Hollywood.

Using field glasses, I examine a slope across the canyon that
burned one afternoon a year ago while I watched from below,
stuck in traffic. In two seconds a tiny lick of flame exploded
into a fire that engulfed a hillside. Today it's hard to tell a fire
ever burned there. Brush has nosed up through the charred
ground. Only the black skeletons of scrub oak show clear evidence of a fire.

Below me a road snakes up from the freeway through the
hills to the west, the future home of the new Getty Center.
The serpentine curves of the road are rather attractive, if you
like the man-conquers-nature thing. Where the road meets
the freeway, construction workers and earth-moving equipment swarm the scene daily. They're erecting a parking garage
and burrowing out a freeway interchange, hoping to "miti-
gate the traffic impact" of the Getty Center, to use the jargon
of the environmental impact report (EIR) that Getty filed.*

Above Getty Center Drive one face of the hillside is
scraped clean of vegetation, except for a few trees I saw being
installed by big construction cranes. According to the EIR,
"remedial grading will be necessary to correct these [land-
scaping] problems." That gouge looks pretty drastic. I hope
remedial grading works better than it sounds.

North of the Getty Center lies an older affront to the canyon, the back side of the Mission Canyon landfill, used as a
county dump in the 1960s. Grids of sprinkler line carve the

---

* Five years later, work crews still swarm this scene as the million-square-
foot, 700-million-dollar Getty Center, now looming over the eastern face of
Sepulveda Pass, nears completion.

dump site into a vast checkerboard. Vegetation is sparse on the landfill except for a thick stand of nonnative pampas grass on the lower reaches of the slope. A little to the north and west lies a subdivision, and a golf course servicing the people of that gated community. (Enjoy the freedom of mountain living—with round-the-clock armed guards!) The golf course looks green and lush. Plantlife responds to the profit motive.

On my side of the canyon the fire road climbs to a saddle on the ridgeline. Against the northeast horizon rise the jagged San Gabriel Mountains. To the east, stretching out below is a pristine canyon; its brushy hillsides plunge four hundred feet to a creek bed lined with sycamores and live oaks. Biologists describe this type of wooded habitat lining a river as a riparian island.

Maps call this particular riparian island Hoag Canyon, one of the largest undeveloped tracts of land in the Santa Monica Mountains east of the San Diego Freeway. The Santa Monica Mountains Conservancy—a state agency chartered to acquire and preserve undeveloped land in the Santa Monicas—says this canyon is near the top of its priority list for acquisitions. But so far the Conservancy hasn't found the money to acquire it. One developer proposes filling the canyon so it can better accommodate a housing tract.

Nearby a coast live oak crowns a hilltop. On my daily commute I've often noticed this tree—a sentinel atop a lonely hill. I strike out for the oak, sit at its base, take a drink of water, and eat some Trader Joe trail mix. Three hundred feet below the freeway drivers surge along. Up here the wind sighs through the branches of the oak. Birds dart in and out of its cover. This is the kind of tree that moved Gaspar de Portolá to name the San Fernando Valley *el Valle de los Encinos,* Valley of the Live Oaks. Today the Valley holds more than a million people living shoulder to shoulder in densely packed, ranch-style homes. Two hundred years ago early settlers could cross the entire Valley without leaving the shade of an oak tree.

Pushing on, I turn another bend in the fire road and discover an asphalt street winding across a vast wasteland of raw dirt. Well, it's not exactly a wasteland. Actually, it's an embryonic housing tract called Bel Air Crest. The bulldozers that carved out its housing plots are what spurred me to take my walk today.

•

In 1978 the City of Los Angeles officially designated the section of the San Diego Freeway that cuts through Sepulveda Pass as a scenic highway. That did not deter the developers Goldrich and Kest of Culver City from proposing the construction of 145 single-family residences and 137 townhomes on a ridge adjoining the highway. As the EIR they submitted states, "no specific plan delineating development controls for this corridor has been adopted by the City of Los Angeles." The report also states that "freeway commuters would experience a permanent alteration in view. However, implementation of recommended mitigation measures should reduce impacts to an acceptable level." These measures include natural colors for buildings built on the hill, landform grading of the slopes, protection or replacement of the trees on the site, and coloring of concrete drains so they blend in with the terrain.

On the ridge to the east of Bel Air Crest, the residents of Linda Flora Drive and the Roscomare Valley negotiated with the developers for eight years over the proposed subdivision. Finally they hammered out an agreement limiting grading and construction so that only nine new homes would appear in their line of sight. Three months later, however, the developers asked the city planners to approve considerably more grading and to raise the number of million-dollar view lots to twenty-nine. No notice of the modifications was sent to area residents. City officials called it an oversight.

When residents of Linda Flora Drive observed extensive grading on the next ridgetop, their attorneys again tangled with Goldrich and Kest and the City of Los Angeles. Too late. Bulldozers had already lowered the hilltop by two hundred feet. The neighborhood groups did wrest an agreement from the developers to raise the ridgeline twenty feet and to perform some landscaping to reduce the impact on their view. None of the residents was satisfied, but as one of them told the *Los Angeles Times,* "You can't really replace something that's been destroyed."

No attorneys represent motorists on the San Diego Freeway. We get the natural-colored concrete drains.

•

I study the landscape ahead for security guards. About half a mile away the road rejoins the existing upper section of Casiano Road, developed years ago. Between here and there a few big-ass houses rise up in various stages of construction. Low plants cover portions of the expanse. As the EIR for this site says, natural vegetation "will be replaced with artificially introduced, though native-appearing, plant materials." Not to mention native-appearing sprinkler lines that divide the landscape into native-appearing checkerboards.

Dozens of pieces of heavy equipment—front loaders, dump trucks, backhoes—are parked at this end of the site. The only signs of movement are ravens circling half-built houses, picking through trash, perching on the Andy Gump portable toilets. The desolation of the scene makes me wonder if we had a nuclear holocaust recently, and somehow I failed to notice.

Along the road a couple of dozen native-appearing trees are

being stored in wooden tubs. According to the EIR, almost all the trees on the tract, including seventy coast live oaks, will be destroyed or moved, and replacement trees will be planted in "groves or in a park-like atmosphere in order to facilitate cost-effective maintenance." At the base of the hill a lavish stone guardhouse has been constructed to defend the future burghers of Bel Air Crest. Around it several large sycamores, which did not have the good sense to grow there on their own initiative, have been installed in a cost-effective, park-like atmosphere.

A signpost now officially proclaims my fire road to be Bel Air Crest Road. Tracing the existing ridgeline (one hundred eighty feet lower now that Goldrich and Kest have taken over its geologic development), the road affords some beautiful views of Hoag Canyon. As I peer over one steep wall at the riparian island below, a red-tailed hawk hops from a bush and sails down over the treetops.

The northern gate to Casiano Drive is locked tight and topped with inhospitable spikes. On each side of the gate a ten-foot cyclone fence marches off into the distance. It looks climbable, but if I hopped the fence I would be descending into the backyard of some solid citizen, probably while he trained his AK-47 on me from his breakfast nook. I decide to take a detour.

Backtracking to the hillside overlooking Hoag Canyon, I step off the brink and slide down fifty feet of loose landfill, landing in dense chaparral. I dust off and crash ahead. In minutes I'm pouring with sweat, scraped in a dozen places, with gnats buzzing my soggy ears. The brush glows with clusters of red leaves—poison oak.

My approach to bushwhacking is simple. When I can't find a path, I choose the point where the tangle looks the thinnest, cover my face, and barge ahead. At this time of year the brush is so dry it snaps away. I'm not exactly a panther slipping through the wilds.

Farther down the wash, oaks and sycamores rise above the chaparral. As their limbs weave together and screen out more sunlight, the underbrush thins and I make better time. Finally I reach the base of the canyon, Hoag Creek. Even in a dry October, water spills down its bed and tall green grass grows along the banks. Sun slants through the big oaks and sycamores arching overhead, their yellow and orange leaves fluttering into the water. To a sweaty bushwhacker, it looks wonderful. Hard to believe I'm in the heart of Los Angeles.

I look for a rock that's not girdled with poison oak. Taking a seat on one, I splash cool water on my sweaty face. Water striders dart up near my feet. With all the sage I just crashed through, I smell like Sunday's chicken dinner. Taking off my shoes, I empty about a half-cup of dirt, pebbles, and stickers from each.

When the rest stop is over, I push on. A serviceable trail crisscrosses Hoag Creek. Here the stream descends a series of ledges. Some of these shelves are less than an inch high; one drops a full six feet, creating a handsome little waterfall.

Crunching through the dry oak leaves blanketing the trail, I enjoy the tumbling waters. The only other sounds are the keening of a hawk and an occasional gust of wind stirring the silvery trunks of the oak trees. Then, in the grass something moves. Black rings around black eyes. Quail. Five of them explode out of the cover and clatter away.

I walk for more than a mile and see no trace of humanity. Finally the woods begin to thin. Atop the ridge to the east I spot a cedar tree, presumably rising from someone's backyard. Then on the ridgeline houses appear, their picture windows gaping out over the woods.

Another fence blocks the trail ahead. Unlike the one up on

Casiano Drive, this barrier proves eminently hoppable. Beyond the fence, the trail is paved with flagstones and curves up along the edge of several backyards. Now I'm seriously trespassing; I want to get past the houses and safely back onto the street. The path cuts through an empty little stable and dumps me onto someone's lawn. Across the yard, staring straight at me is an angry-looking cow.

After a heartbeat I realize the cow is a sculpture. A yard cow.

On the other side of the yard cow's pasture, an attractive woman bundles packages into her Jeep Cherokee, accompanied by her toy poodle. I dart down her driveway for the street. She either doesn't notice me or doesn't choose to. Her poodle eyeballs me coldly.

Back on the streets of Bel Air, the sights and sounds of Los Angeles crash over me. Although Hoag Canyon argues otherwise, times have changed since Gaspar de Portolá trudged through. A Jaguar roars past, then a Mercedes, then another Jaguar.

Pumpkins have been distributed to the houses on this side of the hill too. But over here they're miniature pumpkins—gifts of Merrill Lynch Realty. Compared to Mike Glickman's full-sized sales gimmicks, Merrill Lynch looks kinda cheap.

From Mulholland Drive at the crest of the hill, I survey a grid of city streets stretching twenty-five miles. Supposedly the original Indian inhabitants of Southern California called Los Angeles the "Valley of the Smokes" because its skies were often veiled by a thick haze. I always figured this quaint tale was propaganda promulgated by the Los Angeles Chamber of Commerce whenever the city suffered a smog alert. But recently I learned that sagebrush emits isoprene, a hydrocarbon that can react in sunlight with other atmospheric gases to create ozone, a major component of smog. So maybe there's some truth to the propaganda. Today, however, I see no trace of any sagebrush fumes. The San Gabriels and Santa Susanas, the mountain ranges that ring the far side of the Valley, stand out in crystal-clear relief.

I tramp down the suburban lanes on the north side of Mulholland. From a road called Longbow Drive I see the freeway again. After the serenity of Hoag Canyon, the noisy energy of this river of cars, not unlike rapids on a real river, seems wildly extravagant.

The lower I go, the more people and cars I see, the less remote I feel. Scadlock Lane plunges. The freeway here descends at a steep 5 percent grade. On foot I feel the bodily equivalent of smoking brakes—lactic acid. The muscles in the tops of my thighs burn as they strain to hold me back.

Then I spot my destination, another supermarket, the Westward Ho. From the Bel Air Marketplace to the Westward Ho—four hours—a pace I think old Gaspar would commend. My walk makes me feel a little kinship with the explorer. I didn't exactly map the New World, but after all, how many Angelenos can say they *walked* to the Valley?

•

I had arranged for my girlfriend, Pamela, to drive me back to west Los Angeles. Passing Bel Air Crest and the Getty Center, I consider what I've seen. It seems obvious that all the open land left in a city as crowded as Los Angeles should be preserved for the public good. Yet it's equally apparent that our cash-strapped governments have little money, or little will, to acquire expensive California real estate. We Americans have chosen to live like grasshoppers rather than ants; we fiddle away our summer days, spending our nation's wealth on

Hondas and VCRs, space-based missile systems and junk bonds, rather than preserving anything that's good about today so our children can enjoy it tomorrow.

Don't get me wrong. I don't advocate wasting money to preserve Sepulveda Pass. Even before Bel Air Crest, the pass had been violated. After the developers are done with it, calling the San Diego Freeway a scenic highway will be laughable. That fight has been lost. To understand the scope of the defeat, you merely have to walk the battleground.

On the other hand, my walk itself was a personal victory. It has soothed my feelings about Sepulveda Pass. I used to rage every time I drove through the canyon and saw its newest wounds. Now I feel that in a small way I've one-upped the millionaires and the developers. Soon, when the whole canyon looks like the Valley, I'll still have my memories of a morning spent prowling the hillsides of the Santa Monica Mountains. And years from now, if that lonely oak overlooking the freeway still stands—or even if it doesn't—I can look up and remember sitting at its feet, watching birds flit through its branches, feeling the slap of the wind.

When you live in a city like Los Angeles, you must savor experiences like that. For more than a century, progress in this city has been a synonym for real estate development. Throughout decades of explosive growth, LA has peeled away the surrounding natural world like so much old wallpaper. Yet today I found Hoag Canyon, a jewel buried in the heart of the city—bypassed for a hundred years.

What other treasures lie close at hand? Every day we Angelenos—fifteen million of us—see the wild hills that surround our city, yet we intently ignore them. I hope to be the exception and lift my eyes to the horizon.

Face the Wind

. . . . . .

The wind raps the tree limbs against my bedroom window. I wake with a start. It's dawn. The branches scrape across the glass. The Santa Ana winds are howling. Today is the day, I think.

After living for ten years in Los Angeles, I have developed a love/hate relationship with the Santa Ana winds. Before moving here I lived on the East Coast, and there I was accustomed to weather that changes. Call me a meteorological masochist if you will, but ever since I was a child, I have delighted in fast-moving, violent weather. Give me sleet and hail. Give me thunder and lightning. Unfortunately, in LA the skies are sunny 350 days a year. Here you need time-lapse photography to see the weather change.

My peculiar affection for savage weather is consistent with my overall enthusiasm for wilderness. I'm inordinately fond of eagles, wolves, and mountain lions, although I've never seen any outside the zoo. I revel at the thought of vast, pristine forests, but I don't venture out into them very often. I have chosen to live in Los Angeles and that makes it difficult to fulfill a love for anything wild and natural. In Los Angeles any land that remains open stands as an affront to LA's one unshakable principle: the sanctity of unfettered real estate development.

So in lieu of wild country, which I don't get to see most days, I try to appreciate wild weather. I delight in moments when we humans are forced to accept the fact that, despite the protective glow we might get from living in a city a hundred miles wide, we are ultimately citizens of planet Earth and are ruled by her rhythms. When the Santa Anas howl across Los Angeles, bouncing tumbleweeds down suburban lanes a long day's ride from anything resembling the Wild West, when they peel roofs off houses, flip tractor trailers, and topple telephone poles like tenpins, Nature is merely flexing her muscles. I like it. I enjoy seeing my species getting put in its place.

Of course the Santa Anas are more than just destructive. Most people think they're downright sinister. The common wisdom in Los Angeles is that the desert winds induce peculiar behavior in man and beast. People get irritable. Children grow unmanageable. So do pets.

Some say it's because you can't keep your hair combed. Others blame the winds for carrying positive ions—mysterious charged molecules that function as kind of a catnip for felons. Raymond Chandler, the bard of Los Angeles, wrote, "On nights like that [when the Santa Anas blow], every booze party ends in a fight. Meek little wives feel the edge of the carving knife and study their husbands' necks."

Lying in bed, listening to the wind howling, I throw down a challenge for myself. You say you like wild weather? Sure, it's easy to bleat your beliefs from under the bedcovers. Why not go to the place where the winds blow most savage and see how you feel then? Face the fury of the Santa Anas—point blank.

•

Old-timers say that the Santa Anas blow for three days and nights, and at sunrise and sunset during these days the wind reveals its intentions. If it's calm, the worst is probably over. If it's howling, better not take your Winnebago up into the canyons. This November morning, as the trees rap against my bedroom window, I turn on KFWB—a 24-hour news station. They predict sustained winds of 30 miles per hour with gusts up to 40 in canyons and passes. Definitely, today's the day.

I decide that the point where the Santa Anas are the fiercest must be the 5,074-foot summit of Mount Lukens, the highest spot in the city of Los Angeles. No scientific analysis of weather systems produced this choice. I simply deduced that the highest point in the city is the farthest up in the sky, and the sky is where the winds come from. I jot down a few notes from a guidebook describing a hike to the top of Mount Lukens and set out for the Angeles National Forest, forty miles from my home near the beach.

On the freeway, gusts knock my car into the next lane. The air is filled with swirling trash, including the tragic consequences of that eternal question: paper or plastic? Plastic, and plenty of it, fills the air; grocery bags hover like wraiths over the highway.

A cold front blew through yesterday, and afterward the wind swung around to the north. As I drive through the San Fernando Valley, I see a line of clouds retreating across the southern horizon. Otherwise the sky is crystal blue, except for some puffs of cotton to the east hanging over the 10,000-foot summit of Mount San Antonio, known locally as Mount Baldy.

Meteorologists say Santa Anas occur when high-pressure systems hover over the interior of the southwestern United States and low pressure (like the storm that blew through yesterday) develops at the coast. This unstable condition draws air west toward the low pressure. Streaming over the San Gabriel Mountains, the air funnels through the passes, gaining speed as it howls down into Los Angeles.

Those same meteorologists cannot adequately explain why the Santa Anas have howled so frequently of late. Often during the last few years the Santa Anas haven't blown for just a few days. They've lasted weeks. "A high-pressure system stalled over the Great Basin," shrugs the weather reporter. "It's a normal fluctuation in the weather patterns."

I wonder if the prolonged Santa Anas are a symptom of global warming. The Earth's weather is essentially an enormous system for equalizing the abundant solar energy that strikes the planet's tropical latitudes with the relative lack of energy absorbed at the poles. Scientists cannot predict how this colossal equilibrium reaction will be thrown out of balance by the additional heat trapped in the atmosphere from the huge amounts of carbon dioxide mankind has been belching for the past century. Some climatologists believe that the extra solar energy could magnify the potential severity of tropical storms by 40 to 50 percent. Or it may not. Other scientists speculate that an increase in global temperatures of just a few degrees might tend to exaggerate the Earth's weather, whipping even relatively normal conditions like the Santa Anas into extremes never before witnessed. Or it may not. Divining how the world's weather will react to a shift of only a few degrees is a task too complicated for mortal meteorologists.

Ours is a brave new world.

•

I exit the freeway and start climbing into the San Gabriel Mountains through Big Tujunga Canyon, the jumping-off point for my hike. My ears pop as the car gains altitude. Dust devils swirl down the boulder-strewn wash that is Big Tu-junga Creek. Pine trees dotting the steep sides of the canyon look brown and stressed from years of drought.

Following my notes, I turn down a Forest Service road and drive through a little residential enclave. My presence out-rages the local dogs, who bark up a chorus of protest. I motor past them.

The road peters out near a stand of rushes that marks the presence of a creek. A few willows and cottonwoods also grow here along the banks. The wind whispers uneasily through their branches.

My notes tell me to search for a trail on the far side of the creek. Crossing the stream is no problem; a string of stepping-stones leads across it. But today I don't need them, since all they protect me from is a river of sand. The creek is com-pletely dry.

The stepping-stones are coated with a peculiar, tan, feltlike substance. I bend down to inspect. It's dried algae. The last life-filled pools in this stream succumbed long ago to the re-lentless California sun.

On the far side of the creek I cast about through sparse brush, looking for the trail. I don't find it. I do find a large wooden highway bridge resting on a bed of sand. Its timbers reek of creosote. I can't tell whether the bridge washed here from upstream or if this used to be the creek bed and one rainy day it just filled up with debris.

I start hiking up a steep canyon filled with young smooth-barked alders. The wind rocks their upper branches. Soon thickets block my path through the trees. I try to crash up through them until the canyon becomes impossibly steep and choked with underbrush. It forces me to retreat.

If I'm going to find that trail, I'll have to start over. But from here, the quickest route back to the car leads through the gauntlet of the angry dogs. As I hoof it into the residential enclave, who's sitting in the middle of the dusty road to greet me but a pit bull.

Well, maybe he's only half pit bull. I don't know. I do know he's enough of a pit bull to start my heart palpitating. Especially when he snarls.

I weigh my options. I'm forty miles from home. My car is on the other side of Bowser.

I slowly advance, my heart pounding, my eyes trained on his. He barks but makes no move. I sidestep past his sphere of influence, then back away from him. As I do, a huge black mongrel charges out of another yard. Barking, he tears straight at me. This dog means business.

"SIT!" I scream.

That shocks the mongrel. He stops.

I hastily back away.

I start questioning my presence here. Sure I like a little wilderness, but I also like a full complement of hemoglobin.

•

Back at the car, I decide to reconnoiter more thoroughly and climb a mound of dirt I find nearby. From this vantage point I see the trail marker—fifty feet away.

"Mr. Wilderness," I say to myself, sarcastically.

Soon I find another marker pointing toward the summit of Mount Lukens. Actually, it's just the vandalized remains of a marker; the sign no longer presents any written directions— just some gang graffiti: DEBS. Must be those rich girls in San Marino. Terrible that in today's world even debutantes join gangs.

I start a steady climb up a slope of alluvial debris washed down from the steep ridge that forms Mount Lukens. The debris is all sand and rocks the size of apples. Sagebrush and Our Lord's candle carpet the debris.

The trail switches up the mountainside. As I round a promontory on the mountain's face, the wind slams into me.

The Santa Ana winds are notoriously quirky in their treatment of Los Angeles. An early written reference to Santa Anas, an article in the *Los Angeles Evening Post* of November 15, 1880 (curiously titled "The Philosophy of Sandstorms"), describes the uneven hand of the desert winds.

> We remember once standing at Cucamonga in a perfectly clear atmosphere, while to the south was a stream of sand, like an immense river, carried in the wind storm, passing through the Cajon Pass. It looked as if one could step into it and out, as into and out of a stream of water. Like a swift current of water, the sand stream is parted by elevations, leaving these as islands peering above the sand cloud.

No sand streams up here, although certain faces of the mountain do take an unfair share of the beating. Slapping against my sweaty shirt, the wind makes me shiver. At the first sunny outcropping, I stop for a break. Sitting on some rocks I drink water and study the vast valley below. It's quiet on a Thursday morning. In the distance someone is hammering. And, of course, the pit bulls are barking. Must be another unlucky pedestrian.

I forgot my binoculars. Too bad. On the far side of the valley, in the middle of desolate chaparral, I see a Foto Mat hut. I'd like to determine if I can drop off film there, or if some thrifty soul has recycled the little yellow shack for some other useful purpose—perhaps a spiffy outhouse.

I continue climbing. Soon I'm high above Stone Canyon, a steep wash filled at its upper end with bone-white alluvial debris. Along the trail, the sagebrush yields to scrub oak and manzanita bushes with bark the color of Hershey bar wrappers. Also a few toyon bushes, their berries reddening.

As I climb, the wind grows steadier. I pass occasional ponderosa pines, their bark scorched from brushfires. The wind moans through their branches.

These pines may have been planted by the botanist who is this mountain's namesake. At the turn of the century, Theodore Lukens worked as a supervisor in the Angeles National Forest. To prevent the ravages of brushfires and the ensuing erosion those fires caused, Lukens promoted the introduction of fire- and drought-resistant species like knobcone, Coulter, and ponderosa pine.

On the higher slopes of Mount Lukens, pines are the exception and scrub oak is the rule. It's ubiquitous. Dry oak leaves carpet the trail and swirl around my feet. Rock slides bury the trail. I carefully tiptoe over them. I don't want to drag myself back down the hill on two broken legs. Creatures who are sick or lame make easy meals for pit bulls.

•

I've been climbing for an hour now, and those mountain peaks still look awfully tall. Oh well. I have other things to think about. Should I take that job? It's not the best job in the world, but in this recession any job is a good job. And what about my girlfriend, Pamela? Yeah, what about her?

The tops of my thighs are starting to burn. I think, maybe Mr. Wilderness could handle the pain better if he took a hike like this more than twice a year. Sure, I work out regularly. But that's health club stuff. There are no pretty girls up here to motivate me. In fact, there's nothing at all, except me and the wind.

•

The earliest written reference to Santa Ana type–winds appears in Richard Henry Dana's *Two Years Before the Mast.* In 1836 his ship, the *Pilgrim,* sought shelter in the lee of Catalina Island to escape violent northeast winds. Fifty years later, Southern Californians were calling these winds the Santa Anas. There are many fanciful explanations for the name.

One is that the winds became associated with the Mexican general Santa Anna because his squadrons of cavalry kicked up huge clouds of dust, just as the Santa Anas carry clouds of dust into Los Angeles from the desert. But history fails to record any evidence that the conqueror of the Alamo ever set boot (or horseshoe) in California.

Another theory connects the winds with the Spanish word for devil, *santana.* Supposedly the Native Americans living in the region called the gales that shriek in from the desert the Wind of Evil Spirits, possibly because of their drying effect on berries and leaves. The early Spanish priests translated this idea into *santana,* the devil wind. Experts on Native American languages cannot confirm this theory.

The most probable explanation is that early settlers of Los Angeles simply noticed that the winds often ripped down the valley of the Santa Ana River. City officials of Santa Ana have been complaining for decades that the winds unfairly besmirch their fair city's name.

•

My breath grows shorter. I'm sweating heavily. The shadows up here have an icy clutch, especially against my wet shirt. Often I stop to catch my breath and gulp at my water bottle. I'm draining it fast—should have brought much more than a quart.

I curse Mr. Wilderness for that first hour he spent bush-whacking and playing with the local pooches. I could use that energy now.

As I climb, the folds in the hillside knit together more closely. In the hollows, the scrub oak woods grow dense; they're like full-blown forests in miniature. The trail is kind of miniature too. Whoever maintains it isn't nearly as tall as I am. Constantly I have to stoop to avoid low-hanging branches.

I keep climbing. The summit doesn't look that much higher now. Just another few hundred feet in elevation.

Yeah sure. How many times have I told myself that when I'm climbing some mountain trail?

The wind thrashes the nearby bushes. And me.

Finally, I top the crest of the hill, only to find another crest beyond that, rising considerably higher. The old false horizon. I hate that trick.

•

I keep climbing. Getting really breathless. Have to keep stopping to rest. Pouring with sweat.

At least I'm not suffering from one of my standard complaints about the Santa Anas. Dermatologists say that human skin begins to dry out when the humidity drops below 35 percent. During Santa Ana conditions, the normal Los Angeles humidity of around 50 percent plunges into the low teens. In the hottest Santa Anas, the humidity often dips into single digits, setting the stage for explosive wildfires. I know my skin often feels like wildfire. Almost all skin ailments—xerosis, ichthyosis, eczema (I suffer from the latter)—worsen in these conditions. When the winds start to blow, my skin starts to itch like I have poison oak. Perhaps that's what drove Raymond Chandler's meek housewife to the butcher's knife.

Then again, maybe it's the runny noses, the nosebleeds, the chapped lips, and the headaches. Druggists report that sales of sinus medicines, decongestants, cough and allergy medicines, eyedrops, Kleenex, and ChapStick all soar during Santa Ana conditions.

Thanks to the exercise and the cold, I'm not suffering from a dry nose right now. In fact, my nose is gushing. It's a veritable faucet, and it's completely disgusting. I'm glad no one is around to see me.

•

I see the peak again. Not much closer.

My lungs are puffing like a steam engine. I'm not thinking about jobs and women any more. I'm thinking about lungs. And knees. With every step they go cri-crik-crack.

I used to jog for exercise. Did it for years. What a mistake! I was burning up cartilage—precious anatomical capital—that I would need later in life. Like today. All for the dubious goal of fitness.

I spot a signpost ahead. Keep moving. Rest when I get there.

Panting, I plod to the signpost, stop, and look around.

I'm on top of the world.

Los Angeles stretches out before me—the hills of Palos Verdes in one direction, in another the towers of downtown. Twenty miles to the west the Pacific Ocean glistens. Its shimmering surface stretches off to the horizon.

And the wind is roaring.

That's what I came for and that's what I got.

I'm not quite at the summit. Ahead there's another little hill, not as steep, and on top of it stands a collection of radio transmitters and radars. Evidently a road climbs Mount Lukens from the other side. Yeah, okay, so you can drive up here.

You don't even need four-wheel drive. But hey, what fun is driving? That would be virtually painless.

I push on. "Feet, knees, keep moving," I command.

Their sullen response: Cri-crik-crack.

Fortunately, the slope is now more gradual. My breath becomes more regular. I'm moving pretty good. Until the wind gusts up and almost knocks me to the ground. I regain my balance and stagger on.

Finally I reach the summit. Elevation 5,074. Just me and a bunch of radio towers. Not exactly a wilderness experience, but then neither is looking across a grid of several million people.

I flop down in a little hollow to get some shelter from the wind—that primeval force I had wanted to confront chin to chin.

The radio towers are whining and buzzing as the wind roars through their erector-set framework. I wrap my hands in a spare t-shirt. I need to warm them up enough to stop trembling so I can take some notes.

I drink a ration of water, then dig into my lunch. Cheese, crackers, nuts, cookies, and an apple. The tart juice from the apple tastes exquisite in my mildly dehydrated condition.

Lying in the hollow, I enjoy the sun.

Until I look up. Oh no. A line of clouds is bearing down from the north. What are they doing here? Don't they know this is California?

The clouds pass before the sun. I start shivering.

I could use another fifteen minutes of rest, but shuddering in a wind tunnel isn't really that rejuvenating.

"Okay, okay," I say to the wind. "You win. I'm humbled."

I push myself up, stick my hands down as deep as they'll go into the pockets of my Levis, stagger into the wind, and start striding as fast as I can down from this blasted mountaintop.

•

The descent proves easy. A little pain in the toes. A little pain in the knees. No serious tests of endurance. Gravity greases my path. A third of the way down, I'm warm enough to pull my hands out of my pockets. Halfway down, I drain the last of my water. No problem. I'll get a soda on the way home.

I reach the flatlands near the creek. It's late in the day. The sun has sunk low. The trees look deep green in the flat light. The surrounding hills glow golden. A yellow half moon rises above the valley. Sheltered from the wind, I hear crickets.

One last huge blast of wind staggers me.

"Yeah, I know, I know. You're the boss."

Actually, I always knew. Now and then I just like a little confirmation.

Telegram from God

. . . . . .

To acknowledge Earth Day, I decide to inspect the condition of the Los Angeles shoreline. The beach in LA is the cusp between one of the largest cities in the world and six thousand miles of open ocean. Standing on the tide line looking west, you can stare straight into the eyes of untamed Nature. Meanwhile, behind your shoulder swarm fifteen million human beings.

To perform my beach inspection, I hop in the car one Sunday in April at dawn and drive to the beach near the Santa Monica pier. Walking across the sand toward the waves, I am faced with a scene that makes me think our civilization has but a few days left. We will soon join other lost peoples like the Sumerians or the Anasazi—great civilizations that vanished from the Earth, presumably because they so ravaged their environment, it could no longer sustain them.

On the beach, trash is strewn everywhere. There is so much debris, it looks like a tickertape parade passed this way. Most was evidently discarded by the throngs who flocked to the beach yesterday to escape the hot spring weather.

Walking the tide line, I inventory what I see. One corn cob. Four McDonald's food wrappers. One ketchup package. Five tamale wrappers. A nozzle from a water spritzer bottle. A baby bottle, minus the nipple. Lots of orange peels. A dying cormorant. Twisting in agony, the bird looks like his neck may be broken. Not possessing the intestinal fortitude to put the creature out of its agony, I keep walking.

I decide to make a close inventory of one typical patch of sand measuring three feet by three feet. It contains: four styrofoam cups, a plastic fork, five cigarette butts, and even a little natural litter—two strands of drying kelp.

Continuing on: Watermelon rinds. A used diaper. Three empty Corona bottles. One Bud Light. Another used diaper. Five Miller Genuine Draft bottles. One empty salsa bottle. A tennis shoe. Two seashells. A sock. A comb.

Doesn't anyone throw anything into the trash can?

Grinding up behind me is the beach groomer, a tractor with a giant rake hooked behind it. The rake sifts the sand. A hundred yards of beach and the rake's teeth are jammed full of debris. The driver heads toward a parking lot, empties his hydraulically powered rake on the growing mountain of trash he's combed together, and resumes his Sisyphean task.

The beach groomer is about to ruin my impromptu trash survey, so I hurry on.

A Boogie board, broken in half. A six-pack ring. A Bic lighter. A canned piña colada. Interestingly, this is the only aluminum can I see on the entire walk. What a tribute to the marketplace. The cost of aluminum manufacturing makes recycling cans worthwhile, both for aluminum manufacturers and for people so abandoned by our society, they consider scavenging to be a reasonable career path.

More orange and lemon peels. Citrus peels seem to outnumber seashells. Certainly styrofoam cups do. Remains of another seagull, almost entirely decomposed except for a mash of feathers. A two-ounce bottle of Seagram's Seven. An empty Doritos bag. Five people sleeping under blankets. I presume they didn't wash up here on the beach, except perhaps in a socioeconomic sense.

A sun-screen container. A pink shirt, a blue shirt, a white shirt, a brown shirt. A hypodermic syringe.

Looking around at this landfill-by-the-sea, I think it's hopeless. Time for me to hightail it to the most remote corner of the Earth I can find. With some survivalist training, maybe I can escape mankind's muck for another decade or two. But of course, anyone who bolts like that can't go having children. At least not with a clear conscience. Any young 'uns born from now on will have to face up to our mess fair and square.

One Playtex Living Glove, inside out. Another dead seagull. One Mylar balloon, partially inflated. One red delicious apple, half-eaten. One baseball trading card. Thinking I may have struck gold, I snatch the card up. But it's only Nolan Ryan, and it looks new. Assuming it's worthless, I toss it back down. Disposing of it properly would be a joke. Clearly I'd be the one do-gooder out of a hundred thousand.

A motor oil bottle. A sunflower seed bag. I'm near the Jonathan Club now—the beach resort for some of LA's swankiest citizens. Back toward the pier I saw salsa and beer bottles. Up here I find high-tone litter—tennis ball cans and champagne corks.

I reach the far end of my walk, the channel that drains down from Santa Monica Canyon. The thought of what floats down from those suburbs—packed with cats, dogs, and horses—disgusts me. On a nearby lifeguard stand, a grimy old gentleman yawns and bundles his bedroll. Time for him to move on before the lifeguards roust him out.

As I walked up the beach, I focused my eyes on the tide line (that is, the trash line). I decide to make the return walk with eyes looking west—toward the ocean. This, I hope, will stave off any suicidal tendencies.

With the city at my back, I am struck by the beauty of the morning. The ocean is calm, no swells at all. Perfectly formed breakers roll in. At the crest of each wave, rosy sunlight flashes on white foam. The rising curve of the wave is dark and shows an almost corduroy texture from slight ripples glinting in the sun—until the wave collapses in on itself and thunders across the beach.

Then I see the dolphins. Four, five, six of them. They swim just beyond the breaking waves—fifteen feet from a pair of surfers. On their foam boards, the surfers flail at the water as they try to chase the dolphins. Ignoring the pathetically awkward humans, the dolphins glide effortlessly. Then they flip their tails, send up a slight splash, and they're gone.

A woman walking nearby watches the dolphins with me. We both feel the need to share the joy these extraordinary creatures have produced in us.

"I feel guilty," I admit. "They're so pure and beautiful, and the world we give them looks like a garbage dump."

Right away I can tell this woman practically reeks of a higher New Age wisdom. She advises me, "They come for us. They come to tell us something."

More dolphins show up, four or five at a time, until more than twenty are playing in the waves, surfing down the breakers. I can't take my eyes off them. Such grace. No wonder they bewitched ancient mariners.

The woman stands at the water's edge, waves crashing over her pants up to her knees, her breasts thrust out toward the sea. It looks like she's the one trying to tell the dolphins something.

But maybe she's right. Maybe the dolphins get as much

pleasure from watching us as we do from them. Maybe they don't want us to disappear. Maybe four thousand years ago they enjoyed watching the Sumerians too—until that civilization vanished. Perhaps these dolphins are telling us it's not too late to change our ways.

A thick clump of kelp lies at my feet. Tangled through its strands is a long piece of plastic yellow tape—the kind that contractors and police use to hold back crowds. The tape says, "CAUTION CAUTION CAUTION CAUTION."

Where the Mountains
Run Out into
the Sea

. . . . . .

I've become infatuated with a wild thing.

She is not a hard-bodied California beach goddess. Nor is she a Latin temptress, an Asian mystery woman, or even a prim librarian who lets her hair down in the privacy of her room. No, the object of my desire is a green spot on the map.

This has happened to me before. Because I live in Los Angeles, I don't get enough.

Wilderness, that is.

Driving around LA, I notice the empty places, the unsettled corners of the megalopolis—unsettled, that is, except for the trees and flowers and chaparral that flourish independent of man's devices. I gravitate toward hidden spots where pop-eyed amphibians sing the night away, to lawless lands where snakes and hawks and coyotes kill with impunity—and then eat their victims.

These are my kind of wild things.

My current affair is with Topanga Canyon. Along its lower half—the four miles between the town of Topanga and the beach—the canyon is a twisting, rocky gorge, with just enough room between its soaring walls for a creek, some trees, and a highway. Along this stretch you see almost no sign of human habitation. Near the canyon's upper end, rounded ridges blanketed with chaparral and live oak slope down toward the creek. Occasional houses dot the hillsides.

To enjoy Topanga Canyon, I don't have to make campground reservations and drive six hours to the Sierras. In the parlance of the Los Angeles singles scene, Topanga is not GU—geographically undesirable. In a city the size of LA, smart suitors keeps their hearts reined in until they learn where their fancy lives. Why woo someone who lives a two-hour drive away? Gasoline bills and toll calls ratchet up. Spontaneity plummets.

No, my geographically desirable canyon lies right up the road. Every day I drive it, along with thousands of other motorists.

Although I spend barely forty minutes each day with Topanga (twenty driving up the canyon and twenty driving down), I am so smitten I am pleased to be granted even that small morsel of companionship. For the rest of the day, those minutes remind me that in a place like Topanga I might escape the pursuit of filthy lucre. There, I would not have to go blind staring at photons dancing across a computer monitor. I could reverse my muscles' slow melt into Crisco. Instead, I could enjoy a simpler, more elemental existence: watching the rising sun blaze across the canyon's sandstone palisades; scraping biceps and deltoids and quadriceps on harsh, unyielding rock; tiptoeing through the valley's remotest glens; hearing the whisper of its streams; crushing sagebrush leaves in my hand and smelling their pungence. My forty minutes spent driving Topanga dangle the prospect of personal salvation, of deliverance from a lifetime spent fulfilling obligations to my wallet rather than my soul.

I wonder if any of my fellow motorists feel the same stirrings. I fear they don't. Instead, their nine miles in Topanga Canyon seem to be a race course where they can test the turning abilities of their Hondas, imagining themselves at the wheel of a Ferrari. When I pass through the canyon, rather than wind out my driving machine, I often swerve it to the shoulder. Then I leap out to pounce upon whatever has caught my eye—perhaps a nice specimen of *Ceanothus megacarpus*. To you Ferrari drivers out there, that's a shrub sometimes called big-pod ceanothus, or California lilac. When it flowers in February, its tiny white blossoms powder the hills.

·

Recall, if you can, what it's like to be infatuated with someone. You ache to spend time with her. You drink in her appearance. You want to know everything about her, even the most trivial details, which you commit to memory and then recite back to her at appropriate moments to demonstrate the sincerity of your interest.

You find yourself asking, Who was her best friend in high school? What kind of dog did she have? How does she feel about health-care reform? Stranger still, you remember her answers. Consciously or not, you know that by possessing knowledge of someone, you in a sense possess her.

I've become the same way about Topanga. I want to know everything about my idealized refuge. So I go to the library to read every scrap of information I can unearth about the region. In the car I carry my tree book, my bird book, my wildflower book, and on my daily trips through the canyon I drive as slowly as the frantic driver behind me will permit. I pull over to lower his blood pressure and to give myself a chance to identify the denizens of this valley.

These forays teach me that big-pod ceanothus is the first in a succession of wildflowers that illuminate the canyon for half a year. Within weeks the delicate blossoms of greenbark tint the hills blue. Soon afterward the meadows glow gold when the black mustard blooms. A European native, black mustard was supposedly introduced to California by the Franciscan monks. The fathers sowed it along the Camino Real so that blizzards of yellow blossoms would mark the path of the King's Road as it cut across the trackless hills of Alta California. By May, orange California poppies carpet the hills, often contrasting with blue lupine. In June, the sage on the rugged slopes shimmers purple.

Of course, in most romances the mere recitation of biographical data does not suffice. Eventually, mutual urges lead to an inevitable conclusion. Two must become one. And that is what led me to rise at dawn one Sunday in July and pull on my knapsack.

•

As I turn off the Pacific Coast Highway at California Route 27, better known as Topanga Canyon Boulevard, fog drapes the mountainsides that crouch low over the twisting canyon road. My hope today is to walk the banks of Topanga Creek from the town of Topanga, where the creek plunges into its deepest, most hidden recesses, to its mouth, where the creek spills into the Pacific Ocean.

I plan to avoid the highway. Any fool can tramp along asphalt. Instead, I intend to wade through Topanga's water, sprawl on its boulders, and touch the rosy face of its cliffs. Topanga is a Shoshonean word for "the place where mountains run out into the sea." That's how I hope to end my day, by walking with Topanga Creek as it spills into the ocean.

Unfortunately, as I drive to my rendezvous with Topanga Canyon, I am not bursting with anticipation. On the contrary, I'm tense. For the first mile of my walk I expect to do some serious trespassing.

Now, I don't have many moral qualms about breaking a

law like trespassing. After all, I don't plan to damage anyone's property. I'm not a poacher or a Peeping Tom.

Personally I believe that a precious resource like Topanga—a treasure trove of plants and wildlife in the middle of a city, an undammed creek that flows year round in a desert—should be a public resource, open to all. Money should not grant you the privilege of building your redwood deck in the creek's floodplain, where it will be washed away one stormy day, only to be rebuilt using my tax dollars in the form of federal flood insurance. But . . . that's another story.

The reason I'm worried about trespassing is that the people in Topanga are said to be rather paranoid these days. Too many homeless men wander the highway. Too many Hispanic transient laborers camp out in the brush. I don't want to feel the brunt of that paranoia. I don't want to get caught. By dogs. Or good citizens with guns.

•

Until this century not many humans walked Topanga—at least not many Caucasians. The canyon's early history abounds with tales of smugglers and bandits, mainly because its remote boulder-strewn valleys and sculpted rock outcroppings formed a mysterious badland where outlaws could easily hide. Even today the canyon is lightly populated by Los Angeles standards. Approximately 10,000 people inhabit Topanga's 20 square miles. Most have moved there since World War II, a third since 1980.

Archeological evidence indicates that as long ago as the fifth century, Topanga was inhabited by Indians of the Gabrieleño group, as they were called by the Spanish. A Gabrieleño village was typically a collection of circular homes constructed of thatched willow. Old maps of Los Angeles show that as recently as 1860 an Indian village occupied the bottomland around the confluence of Topanga Creek and Garapito Creek, where the town of Topanga stands today.

The Gabrieleños prospered by hunting small game, fishing, and gathering berries, acorns, and grasshoppers. Anthropologists estimate these people spent only ten to fifteen hours a week collecting the food they needed to survive. That sounds highly civilized to me. I spend close to sixty hours a week gathering my grasshoppers.

Civilization ended for the Gabrieleño soon after 1769, when Gaspar de Portolá passed through the San Fernando Valley in his exploration of California. He was followed a few years later by Juan Bautista de Anza, who commanded two expeditions. These explorations led to the founding of the Spanish missions and the demise of the Indian way of life in Southern California.

Felipe Santiago Tapia served as a soldier under Anza, and after the second expedition in 1776 he chose to settle with his family in California. One of his sons, José Bartolemeo Tapia, was granted grazing rights in 1805 to a rancho known as the Topanga Malibu Sequit. The property was small by California standards of the day—13,000 acres—stretching from Sequit Canyon near Point Mugu to Topanga Canyon. Years later, official surveyors moved the eastern boundary back to Las Flores Canyon.

When Don Felipe died in 1824, his heirs, including his son José Tiburcio Tapia, assumed ownership of the property. Tiburcio was an extraordinary man. While serving as a common soldier, he and five others reportedly staved off a massacre of the Spanish inhabitants of the mission of La Purísima in 1824 during a Chumash Indian uprising. Later, he became the most successful merchant in Los Angeles and served in numerous public positions, including judge and mayor. He also acquired a second major landholding, the Rancho Cucamonga.

In the mid 1840s, when the American occupation of California was brewing, Tiburcio grew concerned about the safety of his gold and silver. He supposedly had ample supplies of both. Legend says he hid chests of Spanish gold doubloons on both the Ranchos Cucamonga and Topanga Malibu. But he died soon afterward. His daughter never found the treasure.

•

I park behind the U.S. Post Office in the center of the town of Topanga and see no sign of an Indian village today, unless those are Gabrieleños living in the VW vans festooned with the clotheslines and tarps. At 6:15 this morning no one in this vehicular hamlet is stirring. As quietly as possible I close my car door, slip on my knapsack, and pad to the creek. The stream is only about five feet wide. With one leap I'm across it, and I start scrunching downstream through the sand.

Finally I am here. Deep in the canyon of Topanga.

The first thing I notice is trash. Lots of it. And pond scum.

Yes, pond scum. It's everywhere. Sheets of greenish-brown algal growth choke the shallow waters. During the summer, as the water level drops in the creek, the scum dries along its banks, forming a parchment-like film.

Next I notice the frogs. I've read that the frogs of the world are disappearing. The cause of this amphibian calamity is uncertain, although some studies have shown that tadpoles are falling victim to increasing levels of ultraviolet radiation. Because the Earth's ozone layer is thinning, it no longer effectively filters ultraviolet light in parts of the world. Yes, it seems the poor frogs could desperately use some sunblock. Here in Topanga Canyon, however, you'd never know they were experiencing a problem. I see dozens of spotted inch-long amphibians. Dozens? No, hundreds. Thousands. Zillions! As I approach, they spring away, turning somersaults in their haste to escape the tread of my heavy hiking boots. I guess I'd turn somersaults too if I saw an appendage a hundred times my size descending upon me.

The creek leads under a bridge where highway 27 passes overhead. The span is a handsome structure, a soaring concrete arch braced by concrete trusses. On a ledge under the bridge sits a tableau of junked couches and tables. It looks surprisingly comfy. The furniture could just as easily have been arranged in Ozzie and Harriet's den. I consider what it's like living under a bridge. Pretty unpleasant, I bet. Cold. Noisy. Plus, there would be all the jokes about trolls.

•

Almost immediately I reach a point where I cannot continue down the creek without getting my feet wet. Call me prissy, but I hate wet socks, especially in the first two minutes of a five-hour hike. Seeking an alternate route to one side, I crash into dense brush higher than my head. Completely enveloped, I can't see more than a foot in front of me. That makes me nervous. After passing the encampment under the bridge, I hear my imagination whispering that I'm about to stumble onto a den of sinister social outcasts. And when I do, they will not applaud my Columbus-style fantasies of discovering previously unknown routes through the city.

I retreat and look across the creek. No way. More impenetrable thickets.

If I want to continue, I'm going to have to proceed *through* the water. I throw a rock into the deepest part of the channel, and use it as a stepping-stone. A couple of long hops and . . . success. The socks stay dry.

The creek bed opens out into a wide sandy expanse dotted with rocks the size of microwave ovens. I pass a car fender crumpled like a candy wrapper by the force of the floodwaters that raged through the creek in February. I hurry past the on-looking eyes of a white Spanish-style house perched high on the bank above the creek. Thankfully, no one stirs inside.

Approaching a green house, where inside a coffee grinder hums, I stride past without looking up. I don't want to make eye contact with any small appliances.

Hopping from rock to rock and tramping down sandy bars, I round a bend. A boulder-strewn alley stretches before me. No houses in sight. I breathe easier. I'm past the inhabited areas. I no longer have to skulk along. For the first time I can begin to enjoy my surroundings. I remind myself to keep my eyes peeled for Tiburcio's chests of gold. Jays honk, protesting my presence, but the babble of the stream soothes me. It's a beautiful morning.

I turn the next bend, and the beauty of the morning drains away. More houses line the creek. Again I'm a lowly trespasser. A deck attached to the first house protrudes far out over the creek. I creep past this first hacienda so close to the porch the residents would have to hang over their rail to see me.

Downstream I discover the chassis of a school bus wrapped around a rock like foil on a baked potato. The bus is huge. Big Firestone tires. Monster drive train. It hasn't sat in the creek long—probably since February. Little scraps of yellow siding dot this objet d'art. A sculptor with a blowtorch could not have fashioned a finer work. Call it "School's (Inside) Out."

More houses. Far too many people infest this stretch of the canyon. Hoping to put some distance between them and me, I angle up through the trees on the far side of the creek. As I climb through the steep brush, I step on a twig. It snaps.

Now, we've all seen this in the movies. It's a cliché. The snapping twig alerts the cowboys to the danger that prowls just beyond their campfire. The sound is unmistakable. Certainly enough to clue in a drowsy cowpoke. You'd think any self-respecting dog wouldn't require a snapping twig to sense an intruder fifty feet away.

But no, that's exactly what the dog in the house across the creek needs. The lightbulb finally switches on over Rover's head. He starts barking.

So I have to get moving. Quick.

Forget the hillside. The brush is impenetrable. I jump back down onto the creek bed, clump down through a sluice carved between sheer rock walls, vault down a five-foot-high shelf, and turn a bend.

Standing in the creek, three Akitas growl at me.

They bare their teeth. I'd never noticed what surly-looking dogs Akitas are.

I retreat.

But not far. The shelf I just jumped down looks a lot higher if I want to climb back up.

Plus, behind me, every dog in creation seems to be barking. Saint Bernards, standard poodles, beagles, Dobermans, miniature dachshunds, schnauzers, Airedales. They're all howling. Even some geese are honking.

I look around. Maybe I can climb up the far hillside.

No way. All loose dirt and slick rock.

No choice but to face the surly Akitas.

I turn the bend and walk straight at them. Trying not to show any fear, I think of what Jack London wrote in *White Fang*. To dogs, "men are fire-makers. Men are gods!"

What I'm worried about is that these Akitas might be atheists.

They growl and advance. I march right past them. They follow me. For a god, I'm sweating a lot.

Forget about keeping my feet dry. I splash right down the middle of the creek. Water gushes in the tops of my boots.

The Akitas close in behind me. I whirl back at them. They dance away.

I race past someone's badminton court strung across the creek bed. A Mediterranean-looking man leans out of his window. From the waist up, which is all I can see, he wears nothing. "Hey," he shouts, in what I take for a thick Italian accent, "this is private property."

"I'm leaving. As fast as I can," I yell back.

The Akitas slow their pursuit. The pack has successfully defended its territory.

I approach another house. A woman wearing a bathrobe leans out of her window. "I'm sorry," I shout up to her. She says nothing. My sorriness is probably evident.

I round another bend and I see no more houses. Panting, drenched with sweat, I plop down on a rock to mop my face and guzzle water.

Now I have some inkling of how a runaway slave felt.

Topanga Canyon has a long and storied history of political and spiritual tolerance. This morning, however, I have seen no open-mindedness among Topangans. I guess I can't blame them for their paranoia. But I find it sad that the vibrations for which this canyon is famous have changed so drastically.

Nearby I see a big terra cotta flowerpot full of some overgrown spikey house plants. I look a little closer, wipe the sweat from my brow, and with a start I recognize it. I ought to. It's a symbol of my generation. Marijuana.

No wonder people up here are paranoid. The spirit of Topanga lives on.

•

If Los Angeles is a city that strains against the attitudinal bounds of the United States, Topanga Canyon struggles against the restraints of Los Angeles. The canyon has long been known as a center of alternative lifestyles—a place where the people are just plain different. While Los Angeles is renowned internationally as a capital of slick, modern design, Topanga seems to have a law that all roadside advertisements must be scrawled by hand—and a palsied hand at that. Some suggest that it's not the residents of Topanga who are themselves so different; rather, the singular behavior of these individualists is caused by vortexes of invisible energy focused in the rugged canyon.

Topangans started down the path less traveled long before the 1960s made it hip.

The first church in Topanga was a Foursquare Gospel Church. Founded by evangelist Aimee Semple McPherson, the Foursquare Gospel Church was a religious movement based on faith cures, sloganeering, and Sister Aimee's magnificent showmanship. Intellectuals scoffed, but in the 1920s she electrified many of the disenfranchised of Los Angeles. The building in Topanga that housed the church was rumored to have served originally as Aimee's mountain hideaway. (There were a lot of rumors about Aimee. Like so many evangelists, she was eventually toppled from prominence by the scandals that swirled around her.)

After several other incarnations, that same building now houses the Inn of the Seventh Ray, a restaurant that for seventeen years has featured what today is called New Age cuisine and ambience. Dining along the stream, you can enjoy a superb roasted Portobello mushroom while frogs croak and owls hoot. The last time I ate there, coyotes prowled a few feet away in the shadowy creek bed. The menu at the Inn of the Seventh Ray states, "Our food is prepared with love from the heart and is charged by our dedicated staff with the vibration of the violet flame for your personal gain, and perhaps transportation to a higher plane."

I'm not kidding. That's a direct quote.

During the 1940s Woody Guthrie lived in Topanga Canyon—in a small red toolshed. At first he lived in a nearby house with the actor Will Geer. But Woody was evidently such a sloppy housekeeper, Geer threw him out. So Woody bunked in with the gardening implements.

During the 1950s, members of the Los Angeles beat generation moved into tiny vacation cabins, built in Topanga after World War I, and used them as year-round homes. The flower children of the 1960s gravitated toward the bucolic lifestyle of the canyon. The musicians Buffalo Springfield, Taj Mahal, and Cream all lived in Topanga. An experimental community called Sandstone located here. It encouraged open sexuality among its members. A nudist camp, Elysium Fields, has operated in the canyon for twenty-six years.

For years two roadside monuments in Topanga typified the attitudes of local residents. One was a huge statue of a peace symbol. It was stolen in 1992. Topangans blamed the theft on kids, or possibly real estate developers. The other monument was the Psychedelic Pig—a wooden porker mounted on a post next to a sign reading "Love Animals, Don't Eat Them." In the '80s a backhoe operator who lived in the canyon revealed, "Topanga has always gotten a bad rap as a hippie haven, and the pig sure didn't help." So one night several of his friends blew it up with low-yield explosives.

Not everyone in the canyon receives the vibration of the violet flame.

•

Once I cool down, I push on. Being chased by a pack of dogs has somewhat dimmed my enthusiasm for Topanga Canyon. I wanted an exciting encounter, but so far it's been a little too thrilling. I guess that can happen when you take up with a stranger. Where are the soaring cliffs that drew me, Lorelei-like, into their sheltering folds? If I don't find that back-to-nature experience soon, I'm afraid this affair of ours isn't going anywhere.

The canyon obliges. From this point on, as I walk, I see no signs of human habitation.

Still abundant, however, are shards of human civilization—mostly in the form of flotsam washed downstream during the winter floods.

A sycamore wears an exotic stole fashioned from assorted smaller trees and bushes, as well as a crumpled dumpster, yellow pieces of siding from the school bus, and a chaise longue.

A hollow-core door firmly braced between two boulders forms a convenient bridge. It saves me the effort of sliding down one rock and scrambling up the next.

Another dumpster wraps around a tree. Evidently, for trash receptacles, the Topanga ranks up there with the great killer rivers. Forget the Colorado, the Brahmaputra, the Yangtze. The big one is the Topanga, Slayer of Dumpsters.

And that goes in spades for automobiles.

A VW Rabbit rests nose down in the creek, filled with sand like a child's beach bucket.

An old motorcycle burrows into a sandbar.

Four cars, including a late-model black Trans Am, lie stacked on top of each other. These seem to have arrived here from the highway that winds along the cliff high overhead. Either the road makes a particularly treacherous curve up there, or this is where the local Mafia disposes of their business associates. I sniff but smell no federal witnesses decomposing.

An old blue VW van is wrung almost inside out.

A black pickup is buried in mud up to the top of its flatbed walls, and weeds sprout from the dirt. The flatbed makes a nice planter. The truck's exposed engine well is submerged in a pool. Water striders dance around the fuse box.

A Checker cab rests upside down in the creek bed. The last fare. It's filled with sand and cobble-sized rocks. The taxi is well on its way to becoming the same type of conglomerate rock that forms much of the canyon walls.

Evidently in this canyon vehicular sedimentation occurs in two ways: cars are driven or cars are pushed. Many automobiles seem to have taken a fateful detour from the road high up the canyon wall. But even more cars seem to have been swept downstream by the creek. They lie frozen in contorted poses, victims of rare days when a tiny desert stream erupts into a howling torrent.

Today, however, the creek is benign. Deep in the canyon, sounds are hushed; even the noise of passing cars is muffled. I glimpse highway 27 only occasionally through the treetops. Along the banks of the creek grow tall, graceful, smooth-barked alders. They are the most common tree here. Farther up the hillsides, dusty California live oaks cast the woods in deep shade.

As I proceed, I'm often forced to scramble over tangled debris driven by flood waters into crevices between rocks or the roots of trees. I don't move with the stealth of an Indian scout. In fact, I sound like I'm loading lumber. With an explosion of crackling twigs, I hop down from one thicket of debris and jerk back. Is that a snake in the sand?

No, it's a shoelace.

I'm a little nervous about rattlesnakes. Consequently, I don't care how much noise I make. Last year I took a short hike in some similar terrain. As I waded through brush, I almost stepped right on a rattler. For anyone who hasn't tried this, I recommend it as the ultimate approach to cardiovascular conditioning.

Along the creek, big rocks are smoothed into jumbled, ghostly shapes. One is a giant white toad. Another's a squatting man. The rocks are made of a light gray sandstone, sometimes dotted with fist-sized rocks, like chocolate chips in gigantic toll house muffins.

I'm carrying a notebook, and I keep tucking it into my waistband. As I scramble down some rocks, the clasp on my pants breaks off. For the next three miles of boulder hopping, I suppose I will have my pants flopping around my ankles.

This calls for a break. I sit on a chocolate chip and sandstone muffin next to a spot where water spills over a little ledge. I empty the sand from my shoes. In a pool by my feet, schools of minnows dart one way, then another. On the sandy creek bottom I spot some sticks moving. Bending closer, I see what appear to be small black underwater praying mantises. To confirm my perceptions, I reach down into the cool water. The creature scuttles away. So does a school of minuscule fish the size of large commas. Later an insect expert I know identifies the moving sticks as *Ranatra fusca*—commonly known as water scorpions. Not true scorpions, these carnivorous insects spend their lives underwater, breathing through a tube attached to their abdomen, which they periodically extend above the surface of the water.

Downstream, the air is dusty from remnants of the morning fog. Dappled sunlight filters through sycamores and alders. I can see up and down the canyon for miles and nowhere do I spot a sign of human habitation, though millions of human beings live within a few miles. I ponder why so much of the choicest real estate in Los Angeles has remained undeveloped. To find the answer, you must look back two centuries.

•

The Topanga Malibu Sequit was the most isolated of the Southern California ranchos. During the Tapia family's tenure, no roads entered the property. The only way to bring in supplies was by boat or mule train.

The Tapia family eventually sold their 13,000 acres, including 21 miles of coastline, to a Frenchman, Victor Prudhomme, who had married one of the daughters of Tiburcio Tapia. Although fifty feet of oceanfront property in Malibu goes today for about a million bucks, Prudhomme was able to buy the entire Tapia parcel in 1848 for 400 pesos. Two years later, however, California joined the Union, and American authorities questioned Prudhomme's title to the land. Unable to clearly establish his claim, Prudhomme sold the property during the panic of 1857 to an investor, Matthew Keller, for ten cents an acre. Keller and his son held the ranch for thirty-four years, and though they did little to work the land, they did legally confirm their title to it. Keller's son sold the property in 1891 for ten dollars an acre to Frederick Hastings Rindge, son of a wealthy Boston merchant.

In the late nineteenth century, the ranch was still almost as isolated as it had been seventy-five years earlier, although squatters had begun to settle surreptitiously in the region. Many of these illegal homesteaders operated under the mistaken impression that the owners of the former Spanish ranchos did not have clear title to their land, and thus it was up for grabs. Ranch owners such as the Rindges fought hard to disabuse them of that idea.

Most of the settlers moved south into the Topanga Malibu Rancho from the Calabasas region along the Camino Real to the north. Major Horace Bell, editor of the iconoclastic newspaper the *Los Angeles Porcupine,* wrote that when a newcomer was spotted in the Calabasas region, the locals were usually "deciding whether he is a known enemy that should be perforated with bullets instanter or a stranger that should be shot on general principles as a possible disturber of shotgun land titles."

In the heart of the rancho, the isolated coves and nearly impenetrable canyons continued to serve as hideouts for outlaws. During this time opium smuggling was widespread. Importers of the oriental contraband would toss packages from passing vessels to be retrieved by men operating small boats out of Paradise Cove, just up the coast from Topanga.

Despite smugglers and squatters, the Topanga Malibu Sequit suited the dreams of Frederick Rindge and his young wife, May Knight Rindge. They built a lavish home, ran cattle on the vast hills, grew citrus, and took enthusiastically to a life that resembled that of the old Spanish dons. But in 1905 Frederick Hastings Rindge suddenly died.

After Frederick's death, May Knight Rindge waged what turned out to be a thirty-year war to keep her ranch intact. Most of her battles were fought in court, but at times violence flared between Rindge's men and the squatters and trespassers who set their sights on the Topanga Malibu ranch. Nicknamed "the Queen of Malibu" by the press, May Rindge was said to patrol her land riding a horse sidesaddle, wearing a khaki skirt and a revolver on each hip. The pistols, she said, were for "snakes."

May Rindge's first battle was with the Southern Pacific railroad, the most powerful corporation in California. The giant railroad sought a right-of-way through the coastal cliffs of Topanga and Malibu. But May Rindge knew that the Interstate Commerce Commission and California law had decreed that one railroad along a route was sufficient for the public good. So next to the seaside cliffs she built her own railroad.

The Southern Pacific stopped bothering her.

Next the Queen of Malibu fought Los Angeles County over a highway. When settlers in the San Fernando Valley and Ventura traveled to markets in Santa Monica, they were forced to use private roads on the Rindge estate. Camping along the way, they sometimes caused damage to the ranch, particularly from unattended campfires. So in 1917 Rindge closed the roads.

That left only the beach at low tide as a route into the city. Rindge fenced off access from the beach and posted armed guards and mounted riders at all entrances. She plowed under all the roads that had been built onto the ranch and planted them with alfalfa. Later, she resorted to dynamiting roads that encroached on her property.

Lawyers handled the squatters. Rindge sued anyone found living on her property. There were many. She spent a fortune in legal fees.

In 1919 the state courts granted the county a right-of-way. Rindge appealed the ruling and lost. By 1928 the county had completed the Roosevelt Highway, known today as Pacific Coast Highway. Rindge immediately erected fences along the length of the highway and deployed horsemen there to prevent travelers from trespassing on the surrounding hills and beaches. Despite her tenacity and all her resources, Rindge could not halt the demographic forces she confronted. Once the Roosevelt Highway opened, squatters could infiltrate her land in force.

The long years of litigation also took their financial toll on Rindge. To raise money, she was forced to lease some of her land, and later to subdivide. One of her first leases was in Malibu to Anna Q. Nilsson, the silent movie star. That was followed by leases and sales to many other movie celebrities. Rindge struck deals with John Gilbert, Clara Bow, Barbara

Stanwyck, and Dolores Del Rio, and in the process she established Malibu's reputation for glamor.

When Rindge and her descendants sold pieces of the land, they imposed various deed restrictions. In the hills, for example, they limited development to one house per ten acres. These restrictions, many of which continued to be in effect until the early 1970s, postponed for decades the urbanization of the Topanga Malibu region. The unintended consequence of Rindge's mania for isolation is a natural legacy for today's Californians: a large expanse of strikingly beautiful land remains relatively unscarred, at least by Los Angeles standards.

•

As I walk the bottom of the gorge, the only footprints I see belong to raccoon and deer. No sign of humans, although I pass a boulder that I could swear was man-made. It's composed entirely of rosy pink rocks, each smaller than my hand, cemented tightly together. It looks like a New England country fence, except the rocks aren't dark granite. They're LA designer mauve.

Until now the hills along my hike have been blanketed with vegetation. Ahead, the first rock outcrops poke through the brush. I soon descend into a narrow gorge crowded with huge chunks of cliff that have crashed to the valley floor. These gray and pink boulders are not quite as big as houses, but they're certainly as large as efficiency apartments.

Highway 27 is now more than a hundred feet up on the western wall of the gorge. Up there I had one of my best wilderness experiences in years. Strangely enough, I was in my car at the time.

I was driving home one rainy evening. This stretch of highway is the most dangerous in the canyon, a mile of steep, winding asphalt that clings to the side of the cliff, with very little to shield a driver from the abyss. I encountered a line of stopped cars. No one was moving uphill or down. Some unfortunate soul farther down the hill had just added his automobile to the vehicular sedimentation on the canyon floor.

Like all the other stranded drivers, I began to review mentally the freeway system of Los Angeles and calculate the odds on waiting. Should I gamble on the road reopening soon, or should I cut my losses and accept the extra hour I'd need to return north to the Ventura Freeway? A few drivers immediately spun around. I had no plans for the evening. Deciding to wait, I shut off my engine. One by one, so did everyone else.

When the last motor switched off, the immense quiet of the canyon swept over us. Just a patter of falling rain. As the last light of day faded, the ridge across the canyon grew black. For miles not a single light shone. Not a porch light. Not a lamp. Not a candle. I considered how a traveler a hundred years earlier felt when passing through this canyon on a rainy night.

For forty-five minutes I sat like this, a traveler stranded on a lonely road in some indeterminate century. Finally, I gave up. My mental calculations shifted. I turned around and took the long way home.

•

As I walk, the cliffs above me grow ever steeper, the boulders larger. Some are the size of two-bedroom apartments, composed of thousands of pink toasters fused together. They dam up a series of plunge pools, which make my traverse down the canyon even more difficult. I scramble one way and face a dangerous-looking leap from a boulder. Besides snakes, I want to avoid broken ankles. Another direction and I'll be wet to my waist. Besides broken ankles, I want to avoid wet underwear. Finally I find a route through some tangled bushes. All the while, my pants keep slipping down—past my hips and beyond.

Overhead the fog is clearing, and blue sky breaks through. This deep in the canyon, morning arrives late. It's 9:30 and the first rays of sunlight are only now slanting through the trees. Songbirds start to sing.

I find the remains of a heavy-duty poncho with a stout drawstring. Yanking the string loose from a tangle of sticks and rubberized canvas, I tie it around my waist as a belt. I like it. One of my role models has always been Jethro Bodine of "The Beverly Hillbillies."

To the east a little side canyon choked with underbrush plunges into the main gorge. Although I see no water coursing through it, the heavy growth suggests a stream must flow here part of the year. The water creates an ecological niche that allows oaks and sycamores to climb far up the sides of this little fold. Higher in the fold the water must give out, because there the trees yield to chaparral. Even farther up the slope, the chaparral disappears into bare rock. Along the top of the ridge—1,400 feet high, 700 feet above the canyon floor—erosion has worn curious little caves into sandstone outcrops.

Once I hiked along that ridge on a first date with a woman. We both clambered into a little birdhouse of a rock formation. After gazing out over the panorama, we kissed for the first time. It was the type of cinematic moment a mere mortal rarely experiences. I could almost hear the background music swelling up. But despite the auspicious beginning, our movie proved to be a short feature. I haven't seen her in years. But, we'll always have Topanga.

This little side canyon is what initially sparked my yen to explore Topanga. Although thousands of people see it every day from the highway, years must pass without anyone forging into its tangled trees and brush. Maybe this is where Tiburcio Tapia stashed the doubloons. Call it return to the womb, call it the same instinct the makes a cat want to occupy an empty box, but I had the urge to climb up into this little valley.

I start the steep ascent. Branches rake across my face. No trails present themselves. Not even a faint thinning in the underbrush. I cover my face and advance. For a womb, it's pretty damn scratchy.

I re-evaluate my urges. To proceed through this thicket, I'll need goggles and gloves. And if I survive this bushwhack, I will still have a long way to walk today.

My taste for adventure is waning. I turn around and descend back to the main canyon.

Ahead the cliffs are sheer, seventy-five feet tall, and made of rosy pebbles, with dimples worn in the cement between each stone. Light filtering into the chasm reflects off the walls and casts a dreamy pink glow over the creek. Sitting on a one-bedroom, I toss a stick into the stream. The little boat races over some falls. Will it make it to the ocean? How often did I do this as a child? How many children around the world right now are watching their boats journey to the sea?

●

As I contemplate the waters of the world flowing together, I realize Topanga Canyon has graced me with a moment when I feel something more powerful than the mundane thoughts and desires that normally crowd my mind. Nature, that siren, has brushed her soft hand over my brow.

But it was a fleeting caress, and once the moment is gone, I am still a long walk from home. As I forge ahead, hopping boulders, I try to calculate how often I have crossed this stream. I'm tired. Still trying to avoid rattlers and broken ankles, I now have to force myself to concentrate on safely placing my feet and hands. My ardor for the hike, and the canyon, is cooling.

Until now the vegetation has been wonderfully pleasant—typical of a riparian island. Sycamores, alders, willows, and oaks lined the creek. But now the vegetation turns into chaparral. The temperature climbs. My progress slows. I hop from one boulder to the next. The road descends closer to the canyon. Traffic noise swells.

I turn a bend and find a young redheaded man hanging his laundry on a tree branch. He is living in a good replica of an Indian domed hut, built of twigs, bamboo, and willow. But he's made one big improvement on native construction techniques. The hut has a sliding glass front door.

The young man looks like he could be a college student. (Summer jobs must be hard to find.) I say hello. He doesn't look eager to converse. Perhaps he notes the rope knotted around my waist and figures, "There goes the neighborhood." I bid him good day and stumble on my way downstream.

Now the stream is all thickets and canebrakes. I've learned the best way to walk downstream is to follow the pond scum. Yes, after a few minutes in the canyon I recognized that pond scum is actually my friend. The sheets of green algae indicate that the creek below is likely to be shallow enough for me to step there without water gushing in over the tops of my boots. Likely to be—pond scum issues no guarantees.

I pass a couple of Private Property signs. Despite my newfound respect for Akitas, I press on. The going becomes even harder. Pick a route. Dead end. Retreat. Pick another route. Dead end. It's hot, I'm tired, and this hike is no longer fun.

Finally I see too many Private Property signs to ignore, and I climb back up to the highway. I know any fool can walk the asphalt, but I don't have the energy to play fugitive. For the last mile of Topanga Creek's journey to the sea, I share the experience with Sunday motorists and Hell's Angels.

Like so many relationships, my fling with Topanga ends ignominiously. Still, I'm glad I made the effort. Although I can't say my morning in the canyon changed my life, at least now I can carry with me a memory of the hours I spent there. I've scrambled back and forth over Topanga Creek hundreds of times. I've stooped to examine the animal tracks in its sandy banks, I've sent its frogs and tadpoles reeling in fear, I've smelled its pond scum. My sweat washes downstream in its waters.

Topanga Creek ends ignominiously too. Next to Red Carpet Real Estate and a restaurant called Something Fishy, the creek sneaks under the Pacific Coast Highway through a graffiti-encrusted overpass. Slayer, TXBone, SPLAT, and Sillie Ting have all spray-painted their runes on its concrete walls. The creek, scummy as ever, drains across the beach and dribbles into the Pacific. Beach-goers daintily step over its waters, not knowing what will float down upon them. They're right to cringe. The creek is not tumbling down from some pristine wilderness. But they have no idea that a couple of miles upstream—practically in the backyard of a million Angelenos—those same waters cast a magic spell on anyone who takes the trouble to find Topanga's rosy rooms of stone.

Tumbleweeds
and Wild Roses

· · · · · ·

The first song I can remember singing as a child was "Tumbling Tumbleweeds." As a four-year-old I would walk around and around my family's little suburban house in Pittsburgh, Pennsylvania—a long ride from the open prairie—and croon

> See them tumblin' down
> Pledgin' their love to the ground
> Lonely but free I'll be found
> Driftin' along like a tumbling tumbleweed.

I don't know how fully the human persona is formed by the age of four, but in my case some personal predilections had clearly been determined.

Lonely but free was an apt summation of my life for many years. I spent the first twelve years of my adulthood working at thirty-nine different jobs and moving eighteen times. (I keep records.) During that time I made few commitments to any individual or organization. I was content to pursue my own tumbleweed-like goal of becoming a professional writer.

Today, however, my life has changed. Two weeks ago I married Pamela, my girlfriend of many years. Presumably that eliminates *lonely,* at least to a certain extent. And when I examine the financial mechanisms now encumbering my life—mortgages, student loans, car loans, health insurance, car insurance, life insurance, disability insurance—it would be hard to call myself *free*.

Still, drifting along like a tumbling tumbleweed strikes the same chord in me today that it did thirty-five years ago. One reason the idea resonates so is that I, like many Americans, was practically suckled on images of the American West. The archetype of the solitary cowboy—the personification of the tumbling tumbleweed—shaped my developing view of the world.

Many of the Western images that molded my beliefs were fabricated by Hollywood filmmakers in a park on the outskirts of Los Angeles. Moviegoers around the world have seen the place. Picture some rugged sandstone cliffs silhouetted against a cobalt-blue sky. A lone horseman gallops before these ancient ramparts. He's riding hard; behind him a trail of dust stretches into the distance. You can almost hear the soundtrack: blaring trumpets announce that this man rides to his destiny.

Those soaring cliffs—they're so familiar they've almost earned a supporting actor credit in American legend—are called Vasquez Rocks. They are named for a mythic but very real character from the Old West, the bandit Tiburcio Vasquez, a colorful outlaw who terrorized California for twenty years during the nineteenth century. The jagged sandstone peaks on the edge of the Antelope Valley northeast of Los Angeles frequently sheltered Vasquez from the law.

I decide to roust some ghosts from my own past, as well as America's, by exploring Vasquez Rocks. Maybe Tiburcio Vasquez and all the other Western characters who have passed that way—both real and celluloid—will appreciate a visitor who wants to sit at their feet and hear their tales.

•

One Friday at dawn I am driving toward the Old West on California 14, the Antelope Valley Freeway. Common sense tells me I should be far from the city, since I've been cruising for forty-five minutes at a steady sixty-five miles per hour. The surrounding hilltops confirm my impressions. The peaks are bony and specked with sagebrush and yucca. But when I lower my eyes, the valley floors contradict my expectations. Every canyon is carpeted wall-to-wall with hundreds of suburban homes, each one roofed with red tile. This is the city of Santa Clarita—108,000 happy folks enjoying clean country living.

On the freeway an endless river of headlights flows toward me. Commuters are pouring in from Santa Clarita and other suburban redoubts even more remote—places like Palmdale and Lancaster, sixty and eighty miles from downtown Los Angeles.

Thankfully, I soon leave the dense-pack country living behind. No more planned urban developments. Just scattered homes. At Agua Dulce I exit the freeway and begin winding through hills tufted with scraggly clumps of grass. Between these patches of life the bare earth glows pink in the early morning light. The wind skips a tumbleweed across the road, and I swerve to avoid it. The song of my childhood comes back to mind.

> Here on the range I belong
> Driftin' along like a tumbling tumbleweed.

•

When I ease to a stop at Vasquez Rocks County Park, the gates are still locked. A rabbit scampers away. I step out of the car, stoop to lace up my boots, then sling on my knapsack.

It feels soggy.

When I left the house this morning, I decided to bring a mug of coffee to ease the long drive. As I walked to the car, my knapsack slipped from my shoulder, falling onto my arm and jerking the mug. Coffee flew out and landed on the pack. The zipper on the knapsack wasn't completely closed, and the coffee funneled into the hole left open by the zipper.

I momentarily considered tipping the pack up and draining the coffee into my gullet. Happily, I didn't sink that low. Instead I poured it into the gutter.

A little java is still sloshing around inside the knapsack. Perhaps by wearing the pack I can apply the coffee externally, through the pores on my back. I need something to jumpstart my morning. I slept poorly. The kid next door kept crying. Some jerk was playing a stereo at 1 AM.

But that was last night. This morning I'm out here in the Old West, and neighbors are nowhere to be seen—at least not at this hour. Hooray. Or should I say, Yippee ki yi yay.

The dawn air feels cool—I can see my breath—and it smells great. Like fresh-mown hay. What is the source of that heavenly aroma? I don't see any alfafa. Maybe this natural perfume wafts up from the thousands of small yellow mustard blossoms that swirl through the underbrush.

California juniper dots the plains around here. Its bluish berries bow down the branches of these clumpy evergreens, each one slightly taller than a man. I pick a berry and sniff it. Doesn't smell like hay. Doesn't smell much like gin, either, although I thought gin was distilled from juniper berries.

Just as well. It's a little early in the morning for cocktails. Spilling the coffee is no reason to start drowning my sorrows.

And right now I have other important matters to investigate. A quarter mile away the great sandstone crags of Vasquez Rocks rear up at fifty degrees from the gently rolling valley floor. They look like a colossal stack of pancakes landing on a chaparral-covered griddle. Their strangely sculpted shoulders and faces glow orange and red in the early light. They beckon.

I pick a trail that leads to these desert sentinels and start walking.

•

As anyone who has spent any time in arid country can tell you, one of its most distinctive qualities is silence. Desert terrain does not generate much sound, since most forms of life there maintain plenty of elbow room. Any sounds that are made do not transmit well across the dry desert air. When a raven croaks, it shatters the silence like a klaxon. The absence of noise makes the desert world seem hollow—almost make-believe.

Some people believe the deafening quiet of the desert may be the reason so many of the world's great religions have arisen from desert cultures. Silence gives a person plenty of time to think. And when you start thinking, dangerous things happen. As America's philosopher of the southwestern deserts, Edward Abbey, wrote, "The desert says nothing. Acted upon but never acting, the desert lies there like the bare skeleton of Being, spare, sparse, austere, utterly worthless, inviting not love but contemplation."

Striding down the trail toward Vasquez Rocks, I expect a haunted, contemplative silence. Instead, I hear the muted but steady roar of automobiles on the Antelope Valley Freeway. In the distance a continual stream of combustion-powered tin cans creeps into LA.

What new religion will be wrought by listening to a lifetime of splattering mufflers?

Within a few minutes I'm wandering through mazelike country that would gladden the heart of any highwayman. From a distance the terrain at the base of Vasquez Rocks looked like gently rolling hills, but up close I discover that the approaches to these peaks are guarded by narrow divides, miniature canyons, caves, ledges, gullies, ravines, arroyos. It's geologically tortured country. Badlands. Perfect for hiding treasures, laying an ambush, or eluding the law.

I veer off the trail and pick my way between two rocky outcrops as big as houses. One is honeycombed with holes the size of beachballs. Between these two formations I find a small cave. Actually it's more of a paleolithic lean-to; a rocky pinnacle has broken off and now lies propped against its former base. I inspect the little den formed beneath the fallen prominence. Pretty cozy in there—if you're a leprechaun.

It's easy to imagine outlaws like Tiburcio Vasquez retreating into these sandstone warrens. To defend yourself in this kind of country does not require tactical genius. Today, however, I hope to do more than imagine Vasquez. I want to hear his voice, know his swagger, watch his mind work, maybe even briefly join his band of desperadoes. This brash outlaw—he claimed that with sixty thousand dollars he could raise an army that would overthrow Southern California—who was he?

Unlike many of the West's legendary bandits, whose stories are shrouded in conjecture and grade B movie fantasies, the life of Tiburcio Vasquez is fairly well documented. Vasquez himself provided us with an autobiography of sorts during his final days in the jails of Los Angeles and San Jose.

Tiburcio Vasquez was born in Monterey in 1835, the son of respectable, land-owning citizens. His family may have descended from one of the first Spanish settlers of California, Don José Tiburcio Vasquez, who accompanied Juan Bautista de Anza in the second European exploration of California, in 1776.

How the bright young Tiburcio Vasquez strayed into a life of crime is open to some debate. Vasquez cast his career choice in a political (and sexual) light. He said that during his adolescence, American settlers were forcing themselves into the lives of the *Californios,* as the Spanish settlers of California and their descendants were called. Attending balls and dances—*fandangos* in Spanish—Vasquez watched the American men push aside the *Californios* and force their attentions on the women. Vasquez said,

> These balls were frequently interrupted, and the participants rudely insulted and outraged by parties calling themselves native Americans. Whatever their nationality, they were a low order of men. From these insults arose my inclination to play the part which I have since acted.

Others say that Vasquez's calling in life had less to do with a budding social conscience and more to do with consumption of *aguardiente.* At an early age Vasquez took up with one Anastacio Garcia, sometimes called Three-Fingered Jack, a fellow with a criminal past. These two and a third companion attended a *fandango* one night in Monterey, where they did some drinking. Trouble broke out and when the constable arrived, one of the threesome shot or stabbed the officer. Vasquez and Garcia escaped, but the third member of the group was seized by the crowd and summarily hanged. (Due process? We don't need no stinking due process.)

This incident hurled Vasquez into the life of a renegade and thief. (According to Vasquez, he first obtained his mother's blessing for his new vocation.) For the next several years he robbed stagecoaches and travelers and stole cattle and horses. His career was interrupted by an arrest in Los Angeles in 1857 for grand larceny (cattle theft). He served a six-year term at San Quentin—not counting some time spent outside the walls of the Big Q during a prison break.

Vasquez claimed that he tried to go straight after his release from prison in 1863, but in 1867 he was again convicted for horse and cattle theft. Clearly, this wasn't his true calling. Vasquez returned to San Quentin to do three more years. On his release he spent some time in the home of a man named Abelardo Salazar, and there Tiburcio's amorous urges seem to have seized the reins of his decision making. Vasquez had always chased the women of California with as much zeal as the sheriffs of California pursued him. Now he became enamored with Salazar's wife. Vasquez allegedly abducted her, only to abandon Mrs. Salazar a few days later. Seeking revenge, the wronged husband caught up with Vasquez on a back alley of San Juan Bautista, where the two men settled their differences with pistols. Vasquez was shot in the neck but recovered.

Many women returned Vasquez's affections more willingly than Mrs. Salazar, though the great bandit did not exactly cut a striking figure. He stood all of 5-foot-6, weighed 130 pounds, and wore a scraggly mustache and beard. Vasquez dressed neatly, however, spoke fluent English and Spanish, and had charming manners. Indeed, he was always extravagantly polite, even while conducting a holdup. During heists Vasquez was fond of embellishing his demands for money with rhetorical flourishes, such as, "I am sorry, but I am in need of money. If you would accommodate me with a small sum I will repay you in 30 days with interest at $1\frac{1}{2}$ percent per month." No record exists of his having ever met these financial obligations.

During the year following the Salazar affair, Vasquez committed a series of brazen holdups throughout central California. Outraged officers of the law launched a manhunt for him, and eventually a marshal happened upon Vasquez on the streets of Santa Cruz. Gunplay broke out, and the marshal shot the bandit through the chest. But Vasquez escaped on horseback—one of the many incredible equestrian getaways he would manage during his long career. Despite being seriously injured, Vasquez rode seventy miles to Cantua Canyon in the hills north of Coalinga, one of his preferred hideouts, where he would rest and heal.

•

As I look around at the humpbacked sandstone forms that surround me, I feel slightly disappointed. I don't hear, see, or feel Vasquez. For that matter I get no sense of Gary Cooper, Clint Eastwood, or even Roy Rogers galloping nearby, nor any of their brethren from Hollywood westerns. So far my seance isn't working.

Maybe it's too crowded here. Based on my minimal knowledge of parapsychology, I conclude that the type of ghosts who frequent haunted houses prefer solitude. Maybe ghosts of a bygone era do too. At this moment no human beings are in sight (excluding the thousands of motorists creeping along the freeway). But this is not the remote hideout Vasquez favored in the 1870s. Visit this park on a weekend and the place swarms with hikers, mountain bikers, climbers, and picnickers. Their presence lingers. Even with my city-kid tracking skills, I can glance at the ground and detect human footprints heading in every direction. It looks like someone used the park to host a huge cocktail party.

That kind of foot traffic is tough on a delicate desert habitat. The ground and vegetation are dry at this time of year. A footprint planted today will probably last until the first rains of winter. Of course, I'm not helping the situation. Every time I see a rock or a gully that appeals to me, I veer off the trail and strike toward it.

Right now some medium-sized cliffs, about a hundred feet high, beckon. I hoof it up a trail that slants along the back of this sandstone iceberg. Soon I'm huffing and puffing. It's 7 AM and I'm pouring with sweat.

Atop the bluffs, I distinctly hear the roar of the Antelope Valley Freeway. Too distinctly for my taste. Humanity is out there—lots of it. Oh well. Maybe someone can chopper me in a cappuccino. The java applied topically to my back doesn't seem to be doing the job. Already I feel dead tired.

Picking my way across bare rock to the edge of the precipice, I find a bowl the size of a large hot tub carved into the lip of the cliff. Throughout this park, rock forms have been smoothed into fanciful shapes by eons of wind and water; most are sculpted with tight, alluring curves. These are tactile hunks of sandstone. I have a strong urge to touch them, sprawl on them, fit my body into their rounded curves. My stone hot tub is no exception. I ease into it and watch the sun rise over the misty peaks of the San Gabriel Mountains. Considering the view, I'd say this tub is vastly superior to most spas in which I've dipped my body—even though this one lacks water.

Between me and the next big rocky peak lies a good-sized valley, maybe a quarter-mile wide. A fine place to set an ambush. Anyone riding between these two outcroppings would be easy prey to a good hand with a rifle. I guess that's why these rocks were nicknamed "Robber's Roost." Seize the high ground here and you can hold off the sheriff for a long time.

A series of four pinnacles rises up from the edge of my cliff. On each is perched a little brown bird. All four sing a lilting greeting to the rising sun. The rapture that I read into the behavior of these creatures does not seem diminished by the regularity of the sun's return. I empathize with the little brown birds. The night around here must get very dark. For us diurnal creatures—sparrows and dayhikers—the blackness can hold many terrors.

The sunrise can be a pretty big deal for me too, when I take the time to think about it. Usually I reflect on this daily miracle—the return of the source of all life—while I shave. Of course, I can't sing a greeting to Sol anywhere near as lovely as the lowliest little brown bird.

Nonetheless, I try. I boom out the first song that comes to mind. "Rollin', rollin', rollin'. Keep those doggies movin'."

From the outcrops across the valley my voice echoes back, "Rollin . . . llin . . . n."

The little brown birds take off. Maniac on the loose.

•

My mother loved "Rawhide." She loved all the Westerns. So did I. We watched Gary Cooper as Sheriff Will Kane. Alan Ladd as Shane. Clint Eastwood as Rowdy Yates. Will Hutchins as Sugarfoot. Ty Hardin as Bronco Lane. Richard Boone as Paladin. Clint Walker as Cheyenne. These tight-lipped cowpokes were my personal pantheon.

I consider whether a person today can exhibit the archetypal values associated with cowboys—integrity, independence, resourcefulness, courage—if you're not punchin' doggies or formin' posses. Do I have to ride the range to live up to those standards? After all, the mythology has already been granted to me; it's my birthright as an American.

I think I do.

And now it's time to saddle up.

Mustering my fading strength, I scramble out of my Pliocene hot tub and follow a path that parallels the descending ridgeline of this great rock. I brush past several round prickly bushes—a species named *Salsola kali,* also known as Russian thistle. This exotic plant (in the biological sense, meaning the species is not native to North America) will dry during the summer months until its stalk finally breaks loose from the ground. Driven by the wind, the bush will scatter its seeds, up to 50,000 per plant, over miles of terrain.

In 1886 some seeds of the Russian thistle were accidentally imported from Europe into America, first appearing in South Dakota. Since then the plant, like many human immigrants, has been wildly successful in its adopted American home. The most common name for Russian thistle is tumbleweed. The Sons of the Pioneers sold thousands of records crooning about it. For me the sight of a tumbleweed unlocks pleasant memories of circumnavigating my childhood home. For biologists the species signals a dangerous disruption in the balance of nature.

Scientists consider another exotic plant found at Vasquez Rocks to be an even greater pestilence than the tumbleweed. In fact, some biologists feel that *Bromus tectorum,* a Eurasian import widely known as cheatgrass, is the biggest ecological problem facing the rangelands of the western United States. This knee-high plant colonizes new territory by means of awns—that is, bristles—that hitch rides in animal fur or human clothes so they can be deposited elsewhere. This colonization tactic has been so successful that cheatgrass now chokes out the native North American bunchgrasses over much of the western half of the continent.

Like tumbleweeds, cheatgrass invades land that has been disturbed, particularly by overgrazing. It grows rapidly, usually winning any competition against native grasses, which tend to grow at a more leisurely rate. Biologists fear the cheatgrass explosion and other invasions of even more noxious forms of plantlife could ultimately transform many of the ecosystems of the western United States into barren deserts.

Ecosystems do collapse. Thousands of years ago, lush vegetation blanketed the Mesopotamian fertile crescent—the cradle of civilization, the land believed to be the biblical Garden of Eden. Because of human practices there—particularly agricultural techniques—today much of the fertile crescent more closely resembles the moon.

My path winds through a field of cheatgrass down into a thicket of boulders and juniper. At the floor of this little valley a small dry wash curls between some sandstone haystacks. I flush a flock of quail. They clatter away and soar into the bushes along the streambed. I follow them down an alley formed of twenty-foot-high boulders—a perfect place for an ambush.

I hear a CLICK. Then a voice. "Stop right there, señor."

I freeze.

What is this? Bandits? Tiburcio Vasquez? What would Clint Eastwood do?

•

In 1871, during the time Tiburcio Vasquez took refuge in Cantua Canyon to let his bullet wound heal, he joined forces with another talented highwayman, Cleovaro Chavez, and a Chilean settler who lived in the area, Ábdon Leiva. Vasquez immediately took a shine to Leiva's wife, Rosaria.

At the end of his days Vasquez was asked if his romantic pursuits led to his demise. He laughed and said, "I have never trusted one [a woman] with information that could harm me." Vasquez was wrong. His affair with Rosaria would ultimately lead to his downfall. But not for three years.

In the meantime Vasquez's daring exploits reached their zenith. He staged so many robberies that the lawmen of central California came to know his modus operandi. Suspecting just that, Vasquez laid plans to relocate his base of operations to Southern California. In the winter of 1872–73 he spent several months around the region now known as Vasquez Rocks.

Before he moved south, Vasquez and three of his men laid plans for what would become his most notorious raid—on the town of Tres Pinos, a few miles from Hollister in central California. They would hold up a stagecoach before it entered Tres Pinos, and, for good measure, rob the entire town.

The scheme proceeded smoothly until Vasquez discovered an official of the nearby silver mines riding on board the stage. It seems that Vasquez and other outlaws of that era adhered to an unofficial armistice with the silver mines of central California. If a bandit did nothing to harm the mines, the Mexican and Chilean laborers there afforded him some protection. When lawmen pursued desperadoes into the area, the miners typically responded to all questions with befuddlement.

Cursing his bad luck, Vasquez aborted the stagecoach phase of the operation and rode back toward Tres Pinos, where his compatriots were holding the townsfolk at gunpoint. But bad luck stalked everyone that day. First a Basque sheepherder who spoke no English or Spanish wandered into town. When he did not follow the bandits' orders to stop, they shot and killed him. Then a deaf man rode his wagon into town. Needless to say, he too failed to follow orders. So he was shot. And when a hotel owner tried to bar the door to his establishment, he was shot through the door.

This last killing was attributed to Vasquez, who was just then riding into town. He denied the accusation, and continued to deny it until his own dying day: "I am not so bad a man as I am represented. I have robbed men, and I have tied them up, but I have never killed a man, never shed human blood, and have always advised those with me not to kill or wound those we robbed."

The gang rode out of Tres Pinos with their haul. Within days, newspapers reporting on the "Tres Pinos Tragedy" declared that Vasquez had led an army of fifty outlaws. The sheriff of Santa Clara County, Captain J. H. Adams, formed a posse and headed for Cantua Canyon, the favorite retreat of Vasquez. But the bandit was too wily for that. Vasquez had instead ridden south for many days, all the way to the San Gabriel Mountains above Los Angeles. He finally camped in Little Rock Creek Canyon, some twenty-five miles from Vasquez Rocks.* Meanwhile, the posse pursued Vasquez down the Central Valley, sometimes riding through the night, tracing false lead after false lead, trying to reconstruct the cold trail left by the cunning outlaw.

While camped at Little Rock Creek Canyon, Vasquez one day sent Ábdon Leiva for supplies—a trip that would normally take a full day. Suspicious that Vasquez was paying too much attention to his vivacious wife, Leiva returned after only two hours and found his leader and Rosaria "*in flagrante delicta,*" as Vasquez put it. The outraged Leiva proposed a duel with Vasquez, but the bandit king fully admitted his guilt and said he "refused to fight a friend he had wronged." Vasquez instead suggested they go their separate ways.

Some historians believe that Leiva's separate way led directly to Sheriff Rowland of Los Angeles County. Rowland, alerted by an earlier wire from Captain Adams, was already

---

* A few historians believe the outlaws camped near Vasquez Rocks, but most authoritative sources, including Vasquez himself, place the bandits in Little Rock Creek Canyon.

searching for Vasquez in the Tehachapi Mountains on the northern edge of Los Angeles County. There the two sheriffs joined forces and, acting on the tip from Leiva, proceeded toward Little Rock Creek Canyon.

Leiva's tip panned out. Riding along Little Rock Creek, the posses spotted Vasquez's lieutenant, Clevaro Chavez, and gave chase. But Vasquez himself, perched high on a canyon wall, ambushed the lawmen and pinned them down with shots from his rifle long enough for Chavez to escape. When Vasquez's gun fell silent, Sheriff Adams mounted his horse and charged alone toward his quarry. But he was too late. Vasquez was gone. As the deputies searched for tracks, they found the outlaws' camp, abandoned.

Again the lawmen rode after Tiburcio Vasquez. And again they followed a trail through the night, eventually arriving at a ranch house in Lake Elizabeth, thirty-five miles away. The tracks the posse followed, however, had been laid not by Vasquez but by Abdon Leiva when he deposited Rosaria at this ranch earlier in the day.

While the posse inadvertently followed Leiva's path, Vasquez was riding furiously on the other side of the same hill, paralleling the route of the lawmen. He beat the sheriffs to Lake Elizabeth, risking a date with the hangman so he could claim Rosaria for his own. The feelings were evidently mutual, because she rode away with Vasquez and they stayed together for several months, while he and his men laid low in the Robber's Roost region. Eventually, Rosaria became pregnant and either left Vasquez or was abandoned by him.

The two sheriffs and their posses ultimately gave up the chase. They had lost the scourge of California. In the following weeks, newspapers reports on Vasquez's supposed reign of terror provoked outrage and anxiety among many Californians. But some of the state's citizens, particularly those in the Mexican community, were beginning to regard Tiburcio Vasquez as a hero.

The governor placed a bounty on Vasquez—$3,000 if delivered alive, $2,000 dead.

•

Down among the sandstone haystacks I look around but see no *bandido* drawing a bead on me with his .44 revolver. I was just imagining voices. In a surreal landscape like Vasquez Rocks, it's easy for your mind to set an ambush.

Imagined or not, I heed those voices, retreat, and pick a new direction, this time toward a large cave on the crest of a ridge that forms the back wall of the park. I choose a trail—one of hundreds that twist every which way—and strike across the chaparral toward the cave.

The sun is rising higher and, despite some overcast, the temperature is too. As I climb I excrete a pint or two of sweat. Nothing major for me. (One of my few natural gifts is the ability to perspire prodigiously.) I scramble up the broad back of a whale-shaped boulder and stride the last few yards to the cave.

Really it's more of a long archway hollowed into the rock. The cave is about a hundred feet wide, twenty feet deep, and fifteen feet high at the point where the keystone would hold the arch together—if mortals had crafted this structure.

The cave's roof is formed from a pebbly conglomerate studded with small boulders, one to two feet across. The boulders protrude from this mix like colossal raisins in an upside-down bowl of bran. The pebbles have eroded from around some of the boulders, and they hang down half-exposed, defying gravity. Glancing around the cave, I see no bleached bones of hikers protruding from beneath fallen boulders. Cautiously I take a seat beneath one of these half-ton headaches. From my vantage point, I hold a commanding view of Vasquez Rocks and the rolling hills beyond.

At one corner of the cave, a dark hole absorbs all light. Unlike the rock formation I sit in now, shaped something like an elongated barrel vault, that hole forms the mouth to a genuine cave. I walk over to investigate. It's a few feet wide, and inside the darkness looks so thick it's suffocating. The floor near the entrance to this cave slants sharply up for ten feet or more. I shout, "TIBURCIO?" The earth answers, "CIO . . . ohhh."

I do not climb inside. On the boulders beside this yawning hole, someone has spray-painted WILD ANIMALS.

What does that mean? Be careful of animals in there? Don't act like wild animals?

Around me countless shards of broken glass sparkle in the dirt on the cave floor, suggesting that lots of animalistic behavior (the human variety) has been practiced here. Candle wax coats one of the rocks I sit on. Over the years much passion has been expended in this cave. Who knows, maybe even Tiburcio and Rosaria cavorted in this spot. Perhaps they would excuse themselves from the band of merry *hombres* and climb into the privacy of the Caution Animals chamber.

I think it's good that people come up here to party and make love. As the footprints trampling the chaparral say, this is no pristine wilderness. If doing the wild thing in a wild spot helps people form a bond to the desert, then by all means, everyone, have at it. I know I feel some strong ties to a certain clearing along the Delaware River and a secluded meadow in New Hampshire. The more human affection for open land, the more secure the fate of that land will be.

Still, people shouldn't smash glass. Save that for romantic evenings by the fireplace. Or arguments in the kitchen.

•

Descending from the cave, I follow a path toward a section of the park I have not yet explored. Although Vasquez Rocks County Park consists of only 745 acres, it's easy to lose your orientation here. Throughout the park the trails rise and fall, twist and turn. Often as not, massive rock outcroppings block your view. When I lose my way, I simply shed a few ounces of sweat and climb the nearest rock formation. Once I gain some altitude, I can survey the topography and recover my bearings.

Soon the trail leads me down a little wash, dry now, but evidently wet not many weeks ago. My eyes follow the streambed up a little fold in the rocks to a U-shaped lip, stained dark from water that cascades over it during the wet season. Every year the U is carved deeper.

Nearby I spot a small cave, about six feet in diameter, and I check inside. I always inspect hidey-holes like this, just in case they hold hidden treasure.

No booty stashed in this little grotto. Unless you treasure creatures with long floppy ears. A rabbit currently inhabits the hole. It pants heavily as it stares out at a life-threatening monster: Me.

The path leads me away from the dry wash and up a small ridge. At the crest, I can see into the next valley, which holds a glade of sycamores sheltering a small stream. The dense green vegetation proves a soothing balm to my eyes, strained after two hours of glaring sandstone.

The trail winds down to the stream. This is Escondido Creek—six feet wide, six inches deep. The oasis it creates must have looked like paradise to any traveler a hundred years ago who just humped it here on foot from the Mission San Fernando, fifteen miles away. Or maybe Lancaster, twenty-five miles across the Mojave Desert.

Under the full brunt of the California summer, the creek is

shrinking. Pond scum now chokes its shallower pools; moss covers the rocks. Down in this glade you'd never know you were perched on the edge of the Mojave. The air feels cool and wondrously damp. Along the creek's banks, coastal sage grows rampant. Earlier I passed clumps of sage clinging to the exposed hillsides of the park. With the winter's wet weather now six weeks gone, those stands of sagebrush were drying out. Yellow tinted their threadlike leaves. But in this island of moisture along Escondido Creek the sage still glows a luminous white-green.

A few hundred yards downstream a grove of big sycamores arches over the creek. They draw me like a magnet. I seem to suffer from a mysterious malady: I'm attracted to trees. I don't mean scrub brush, or ornamental fruit trees, or even most kinds of palms. It's big trees I like, with sturdy trunks and broad, spreading limbs. What draws me is not the allure of the tree's cool shade—nor any of its other tangible qualities. My compulsion seems far more instinctive. Perhaps it's a behavioral vestige of my monkey ancestors.

Approaching those sycamores from my side of the creek looks impossible. The banks are too steep, the brush too thick. But the chaparral on the far side appears a little thinner. Using my walking stick, I vault the creek and wade into the thickets. After a few steps I'm doing serious bushwhacking. Holding my hands high over my head so they won't get scratched, I bulldoze ahead, leading with my chest. The brush responds with solid blows to my midsection.

This reminds me of another chapter in the life of Tiburcio Vasquez, an epic saga in the annals of bushwhacking.

•

Several months after he escaped from the two posses, Vasquez returned to his old hideout in Cantua Canyon and continued playing his self-described part in life. He gathered some new recruits and staged several more daring holdups.

The governor raised the bounty on Vasquez: $8,000 alive, $6,000 dead. He also allocated $5,000 to recruit what was essentially an All-Star Posse.

Led by Sheriff Harry Morse, this team included four other lawmen and four volunteer citizens. Sheriff Tom Cunningham of Stockton, nicknamed "The Thiefcatcher of San Joaquin," joined the posse. (In those days everyone had nicknames.) Cunningham called the posse's journey "the hardest riding I ever saw. We covered 2,709 miles, an average of 45 and one-half miles per day during the sixty days we were out. The chase led us through Fresno, Monterey, Tulare, San Luis Obispo, Kern, and Los Angeles Counties."

Vasquez, meanwhile, had moved back to the Vasquez Rocks region, where he planned yet another campaign. During his career, Vasquez often drew on help from Mexican-Americans living throughout California. Acting on a tip from one of these sympathizers, Vasquez now targeted an Italian rancher named Repetto in San Gabriel. Pretending to be sheep-shearers in search of work, Vasquez and his men entered Repetto's house, tied up the rancher, and demanded money—lots of it—because Vasquez had learned from his source that the rancher had recently sold $10,000 worth of sheep. Repetto protested that he had paid out all that money for bills. Vasquez insisted on examining the books for himself.

When Repetto surrendered his records, Vasquez studied them and realized the man's claims were true. He then politely requested that Repetto send his nephew to a bank in Los Angeles to secure a small "loan" of $800 for Vasquez. The rancher kindly obliged.

In Los Angeles, the nephew alerted Sheriff Rowland, and

within a half hour the sheriff had formed a posse led by Under-sheriff Johnson. Vasquez's men spotted the approaching posse and fled. With fresh horses, they soon outdistanced Johnson. After pausing in the Arroyo Seco to relieve three travelers of their cash and jewelry, Vasquez and his men rode into the winding canyons of the San Gabriels. They intended to follow a surveyor's road across the mountains into Big Tujunga Canyon, a region where they had often taken refuge. But to their shock, the road abruptly ended. A huge ridge blanketed with dense, seemingly impenetrable chaparral separated the bandits from the safety of Big Tujunga. The ridge before them included the highest point for miles around—a peak later named Mount Lukens.

With Johnson's posse bearing down from behind, Vasquez and his men had no choice. They forged ahead.

The powerfully built Chavez led the way, breaking through dense manzanita thickets and scrub oak forests, scrambling across steep, wooded gulches. The others followed on foot, their horses behind them. Hours of crashing, hacking, and clawing advanced them only a few hundred yards. Fortunately for Vasquez, Johnson's men now confronted the same obstacles—not to mention the fear of ambushers lurking in the dense thickets.

After slashing through brush for hours, under hot sun and without water, Vasquez and his men topped the ridge and chose a route down a steep gulch. It seemed almost impossible that a horse could traverse this descent. Chavez, however, mounted his animal and spurred it down the plummeting hillside. With a scream the horse fell to its death. Chavez leapt to safety at the last instant.

Vasquez and the others led their horses more carefully down the precipice. They succeeded, only to discover that they now stood at the top of a waterfall, completely impassable for horses. The bandits abandoned their mounts and continued on foot.

Eventually Vasquez and his men reached the floor of Big Tujunga Canyon. They knew several Mexicans there who offered them food, shelter, and horses. Over the next few days Vasquez and his men escaped, one by one, from Tujunga Canyon. They had eluded the law again. But not for long.

•

After gaining a few yards crashing through my own sagebrush thickets, I conclude that Vasquez and Chavez were far more motivated than I. My life does not depend on this brambly passage. For that matter, neither does my hike. Today I'm conducting a seance for some Western ghosts. I can gambol under sycamore trees another day. So I sound the retreat.

On this hike I've been carrying a walking stick, which I recently received as a gift. I use the stick to vault back across the stream. A walking stick is a wonderful thing. The stream may be only six feet wide, but without my staff, springing six feet from a standstill is more than I can manage. And dry socks are, of course, a thing to be cherished.

On the other side of the stream I soon encounter a sign claiming this path as part of the Pacific Crest Trail, a superhighway for backpackers, stretching 2,400 miles from Mexico up the spine of the Sierras and Cascades all the way to Canada.

After a few yards I spot an inviting boulder overlooking the creek and take a seat on its lip. The morning sun is still low; it casts long shadows across the glen and suffuses the lush foliage with a vibrant green glow.

I consider whether I would be out here hiking by myself if not for all those cowboy songs I sang as a kid, or all those

Western movies I watched. What does a guy do when he, like Shane, hears the call of the faraway hills? Become a long-haul truck driver? A forest ranger? Half of them wear bullet-proof vests to work. How much work would an upright guy like Paladin find today by peddling his gun and his willingness to travel? My guess is: not much. Our world offers few honest ways to distinguish yourself as a rugged individualist.

As if on cue I hear a clumping from upstream. A heavily burdened hiker turns the bend. Judging from his backpack, which is bundled high as his hat, this fellow is traveling a long way. We nod to each other, and after he passes my thoughts tramp down the trail behind him.

I wonder where the backpacker is bound. Maybe it's time for me to strap on the real pack—not my daypack but the big REI Expedition model—and follow this hiker. By autumn I'd be in British Columbia. Of course, the first few days, crossing sixty miles of Mojave Desert with only a gallon of water, could be challenging.

I fight the urge for a minute.

Why the hell not? Who'd care?

Well, my new wife, for one.

I could send her a postcard.

•

I don't follow the backpacker.

It's true. I am not a tumbling tumbleweed.

Instead I continue south on the Pacific Crest Trail. And despite the fact that this is probably one of the best-marked trails in America, I promptly lose my way.

Time to shed some saltwater.

I start climbing. This rock is a big one. I'm huffing, puffing, squeezing a few more calories of energy from my reluctant body. When I finally reach the summit, I see Bedrock.

No, not some igneous or metamorphic strata. Bedrock with a capital B. The home of Fred Flintstone. Preferred address for any modern Stone Age family.

It's a movie set for the film *The Flintstones,* and it's so realistic the cartoon of my youth seems to have sprung to life. The artistry (and vast quantities of money) applied to this mock-up are remarkable.

Yes, Vasquez Rocks are performing their traditional role as a backdrop for America's fantasies. Only this isn't a myth of the old West. It's a myth of the very very very old West.

Over the decades dozens of movies and television shows have been filmed at Vasquez Rocks: "Bonanza," "F Troop," *The Girl and the Gambler, The Far Frontier, Young Buffalo Bill* (starring Roy Rogers and Gabby Hayes), *Apache Rose* (directed by the noted action auteur William Witney), *The Conquest of Cochise* (described in *Western Films: A Complete Guide* as "Charming love-the-ladies cavalry major tries to make peace with Apache leader Cochise despite racial tensions and melodramatic machinations by crude villains"), *The Gallant Legion* ("Texas Ranger fights off a gang of opportunists who want to split Texas up into five pieces"), and *The Legend of the Lone Ranger* ("utterly asinine"). Vasquez Rocks has also served as a backdrop for science fiction shows, including "Flash Gordon," "Star Trek," and the ever-popular *Amazon Women on the Moon.*

Crowds of people are streaming down the main road of the park toward Bedrock. I can't tell whether these are extras for a filming or sightseers touring a neo-prehistoric fantasy. In any case, I'm not quite ready for a wave of humanity. I still need a few words with Tiburcio.

Instead of following the soft dirt trail toward Bedrock (yabba dabba doo), I turn left and scramble up another rocky slope (*ándale, ándale*).

Soon I cross a field dotted with the stalks of Our Lord's candle. This peculiar plant bears a fruit resembling a small green pepper. It reproduces by means of a unique symbiosis with the California yucca moth. The female moth gathers a ball of pollen at one flower, carries it to another flower, makes a hole in the pistil, deposits her eggs in the hole, and places the ball of pollen on top of the pistil. When the eggs hatch, the caterpillars emerge, eat some of the pistil, spin a thread to lower themselves to the ground, and bury themselves near the plant. They emerge a year later as moths.

I lope down one hill, then up another rise, then down, then up, all the while winding through cheatgrass, buckwheat, juniper, and chamise. As I scramble up and down these little ridges, my toes pound against the front of my stiff boots. My tootsies are starting to hurt. I've had these boots only seven years, so they're not quite broken in.

The day is getting good and hot. Occasionally I pause in small wedges of shade cast by a juniper or chamise. Down in the little valleys, it's quiet. Like the real desert. No freeway noise here. The only sounds are the wind sighing through the juniper branches and a few birdcalls.

Finally my path leads me to the foot of the highest rock formation in the park—a fortress of large, rounded, jumbled stones. What do they remind me of? I think for a minute. I know. Little suburban caveman houses. Ah ha! See how insidious Hollywood is. They need only a few minutes to seize control of your brain waves.

I start ascending. Almost all the rock formations in Vasquez Rocks County Park are eminently climbable. That's why these rocks swarm with humanity every weekend. They don't take mountaineering skill. Just perspiration.

By the time my brow drips, I am nearing the summit. I circle through some boulders as big as kitchens—another good place for an ambush—then clamber toward the peak, a smooth, steep, pyramidal boulder. I creep up on all fours. At the top, I rise to my feet and can see twenty miles or more in every direction. I stand on the throne of the bandit king.

In the distance, range after range of mountains rise into the haze. In the foreground, massive rock formations stud the landscape. They look like the ribs of the earth jutting straight up into the air. Standing atop them stirs your spirit. Maybe that is one reason Tiburcio favored this country.

When I look toward the front gate of the park, I see a continual stream of humans pouring in to tour Bedrock. Beyond the gate, on the other side of the highway, suburban houses dot the rolling hills. That way, I conclude, lies the land of fantasy—Hollywood fantasy and, even worse, real estate fantasy. Clean country living is spreading like gangrene through these rugged badlands. The first symptom is a red-tiled roof.

I choose to look in the other direction, at what I consider the real world. (I take the long view, the geologic view.) In a few eons those red-tiled roofs—like most other human follies and blights—will pass. The rocks will remain.

•

In a curious intersection of fact and fantasy, Tiburcio Vasquez met his fate in Hollywood. Only in 1874 that part of town was called Rancho La Brea.

When Vasquez fled Tujunga Canyon, he took refuge for more than a week at the home of a man called Greek George. George was actually a Syrian camel-driver brought to America by the Confederacy during the Civil War as part of an ill-fated attempt to use camels in the southwestern deserts. Evidently, to most Americans of that day, a Syrian was the same as a Greek. Vasquez and his men had often enjoyed the hospitality of Greek George's home, located at the base of what is now called the Hollywood Hills.*

While Vasquez rested, Sheriff Morse was leading his tired posse north to Alameda County. At Fort Tejon, however, they received a tip that Vasquez was holed up at Greek George's. Since this location was squarely in Sheriff Rowland's jurisdiction, Morse took the stage to Los Angeles to pass on the information. But Rowland discounted the informant, and Morse resumed his journey north.

Meanwhile, Rowland set about claiming his undivided share of the $8,000 bounty. He chose eight men. Each traveled separately to the Rancho La Brea, so as not to arouse any suspicions. Assuming positions in the hills above George's house, the lawmen studied the site for hours. To storm the house looked perilous. But then they spotted two Mexican woodcutters leading a wagon that would pass near Greek George's. The deputies commandeered the wagon, concealed six men in its box, and warned the Mexicans not to reveal that anything was amiss—or each would feel a bullet in his brain. When the woodcutters neared George's homestead, the lawmen rolled off it, stole into nearby thickets, and surrounded the house.

Peering inside, they saw Vasquez eating dinner. The wife of Greek George caught sight of them, screamed, and tried to bar the door. Vasquez dived out a window. One deputy fired a shotgun blast at him and missed. Outside, another lawman shot at Vasquez, hitting him in the shoulder. The king of the outlaws saw he was surrounded and threw up his arms.

The city of Los Angeles reacted to the capture of Vasquez

* Greek George's house stood at what today is the corner of Kings Road and Fountain Avenue, an undistinguished mishmash of apartment buildings and condominiums.

with jubilation. Schools were dismissed so students could join in the celebration. As Vasquez sat in the Los Angeles jail, swarms of visitors descended upon him, most of them women, many from the higher strata of society. The notorious bandit was showered with flowers, wine, and other gifts. In return Vasquez treated all with his customary gracious manners.

Vasquez was transported to San Jose for trial. Due largely to the testimony of Ábdon Leiva, Vasquez was convicted of murder for the killings at Tres Pinos and sentenced to die by hanging. As the date of the execution neared, rumors abounded in San Jose that bands of armed Mexicans were marching to rescue Vasquez.

None arrived.

All who witnessed the execution on March 19, 1875 said Tiburcio Vasquez faced the hangman's noose with as much fortitude as any man ever confronted his own death. When the executioner placed the black hood over his head, Vasquez's final word was "Pronto!"

•

As I stand atop Vasquez Rocks, cool, delicious, invigorating air roars in from the north. Swallows dart and dive in the breezes around my head. The birds seem to exult in the beauty of the moment and their freedom to enjoy it.

Tiburcio was onto something here in these rocks. Was Vasquez a good guy or a bad guy? I don't know. I'll leave that decision to the Hispanic-rights advocates, the Western law-and-order buffs, and everyone else who wants to promote their own agenda by reinterpreting history. Probably Vasquez was both. In any case, he was certainly strong, independent, resourceful, and courageous.

He was, in short, a rugged individualist. And unlike many

so-called legends of the American West, Vasquez was not a product of Hollywood scriptwriters. On the contrary, his was the type of life that would provide inspiration to later generations of writers and filmmakers. Like garden roses bred from the seeds of some wild strain, our mass-produced Hollywood legends are the sanitized offspring of men like Tiburcio Vasquez.

And so I thank this Latino bandit for inspiring me, albeit indirectly, to stand on the summit of a peak named after him, feeling the cool air race over me and watching the swallows play.

•

I walk down from my peak and stroll back to my car via the streets of Bedrock. I survey the Stone Age porticos constructed of tyrannosaurus bones, the television antennas fashioned of twigs. The set's a beauty. I examine the internal workings of a lifelike mechanical brontosaurus—a simulation of Jurassic life, ingeniously powered by pulleys and counterweights. I dodge a string of fifteen pre-school children walking in a row holding hands.

As I drive away from the park, I pass the Hacienda Vasquez Adult Mobile Home Park. The legend lives on.

Thus Speaks Zeus

. . . . . .

When I was born my father planted two maple saplings in the front yard of our house. With that act, John Wicinas, a Lithuanian steelworker in Pittsburgh, continued a human tradition more than two thousand years old.

When the Roman poet Virgil was born in 70 BC, his family planted a poplar tree in his honor. When a child was born to Pacific Islanders, they traditionally planted a coconut palm. The number of growth rings on its bark was said to foretell the years the child would live. When a son was born to Muhammad the Conqueror, the Ottoman ruler who overran southern Europe in the fifteenth century, the great sultan planted a plane tree in honor of his boy. It lived 400 years. Throughout the centuries humans have believed that the flourishing of these commemorative trees portends the well-being of the child. If the tree weakens or dies, the child may too.

I think of our two maple trees in Pittsburgh as I lie on my back at the foot of a fifty-foot-tall Engelmann oak in western Riverside County, ninety miles from my home in Los Angeles. Those maples matured alongside me. In the summer I played in the cool shade they cast over our front porch; in winter I stood in our living room and watched their bare limbs claw at the wind. As the two trees grew, they gradually enfolded our little house into their widening arms.

Recently I visited that house. Years had passed since my family had lived there, and as I turned the last bend before its yellow brick walls came into view, I held my breath, dreading to see the condition of the two maples. To my relief, both stood tall and robust. Perhaps my days are not yet numbered.*

For reasons far more complex than being reared in the shade of two big sugar maples, I have always felt a deep attraction to trees—big trees with stout trunks that stand for centuries, branches that arch to the sun, and leaves that shade you and whisper secrets when the breeze stirs. I do not much care for lollipop-shaped ornamentals or scraggly, fast-growing weed trees. And I especially don't like the symbol of Los Angeles—the palm, which to me looks like a giant toilet brush and offers little value other than some interesting visual design qualities. No, I love what I call real trees. Sycamores, hickories, and beeches. Maples, elms, and oaks. And I am not alone. For tens of thousands of years, those types of trees have captured the human imagination.

In the nineteenth century the state of California gained a reputation as a paradise. This was not simply because mild weather blessed the state, or because settlers stumbled onto

---

* As I write these last words, I ensure my presumed good luck by knocking on wood. This widespread superstition supposedly guarantees good fortune either by honoring the wood of the cross upon which Christ was crucified or the wood of trees that ancient European cultures considered sacred. An alternative explanation theorizes that knocking on wood prevents malicious spirits that may be present—perhaps in the wood itself—from hearing of my good fortune and having their jealousy so aroused that they might seek to dash my good luck. Be it Christ, Druids, or supernatural beings in a snit, I knock wood religiously.

gold in the Sierra foothills. At the time, much of California was dominated by an ecosystem that people found deeply appealing. Vast, grassy hills and plains blanketed much of the state, interspersed with stands of majestic oaks. When the English explorer George Vancouver visited California in 1796, he wrote of the Santa Clara Valley:

> It could only be compared to a park which had been closely planted with the true old English oak; the underwood that had probably attended its early growth had the appearance of having been cleared away and left the stately lords of the forest in complete possession of the soil.

In 1844 John C. Frémont described the land near the American River:

> The country is smooth and grassy; the [woodlands] had no undergrowth; and in the open valleys of rivulets, or around spring heads, the low groves of oak give the appearance of orchards in an old cultivated country.

Today, little of this landscape endures, especially in the southern half of the state. One remnant, though, survives in Riverside County, amid the suburban sprawl that radiates from Los Angeles. The Santa Rosa Plateau Ecological Reserve is a tract of land owned and operated by the Nature Conservancy, a private organization dedicated to preserving threatened ecosystems around the world. The reserve's seven thousand acres of rolling grasslands and oak woodlands serve as a modern-day Noah's ark for many species of California's plants and animals. There, many organisms, including *Homo sapiens,* can take refuge from the rising tide of asphalt, concrete, and stucco that has inundated most of Southern California.

The predominant tree on the Santa Rosa Plateau is the

Engelmann oak, often called the most endangered tree in California. Although never widespread in modern times, the Engelmann oak once grew throughout Southern California and flourished near the cities of Pomona and Pasadena. The tree was sometimes known as the Pasadena oak. At the turn of the century the image of the Engelmann oak came to symbolize the Arts and Crafts Movement, centered in Pasadena. Artists of that era often depicted Engelmann oaks, with their distinctive, outstretched, angular limbs, in ceramics, decorative woodwork, stained glass, and graphic designs. Today, LA's explosive growth has obliterated all but a few of the Engelmann oaks in the Pasadena vicinity. The tree's range is now limited to two significant stands—one in San Diego County and one on the Santa Rosa Plateau.

Lying at the foot of that huge Engelmann oak on the Santa Rosa Plateau, I stretch out on a big boulder. I listen to woodpeckers hammer in the distance, watch the branches sway overhead. Today I want to explore the *idea* of trees. I want to calculate their worth. Not in board feet but as brethren, as fellow travelers on a journey lasting millennia, shipmates on an ark much larger than the Santa Rosa Plateau.

●

I arrive at the Santa Rosa Plateau on a December morning just as the sun starts to burn through a dense layer of fog. From the heated comfort of my car, I step out into cold gray air and the liquid song of meadowlarks.

I pull on my knapsack, poke my hands deep in my pockets, and start down a narrow dirt trail that cuts through a field of wet grass. Fog blurs the edges of this world. The horizon seems a vague demarcation between gray heavens and gray earth. Shadowy sycamores loom over me. A tapping noise rings from the leaves; it sounds like light rain but is actually heavy dew dripping from leaf to leaf. On both sides of the trail the straw-colored grass is dyed dark brown from all the moisture. Scattered across the field are thousands of spiderwebs. Dripping with dew, they sparkle like the last stars of dawn.

The trail soon winds past an oak. Its branches are twisted, its bark covered with lichen. The leaves are a muted blue-green; this tree doesn't look like any oak I've ever seen.

Oaks are rampant hybridizers and difficult to identify positively by any single trait, so I pull my oak identification guide from my pack. For the Engelmann oak it says: "Leaves are blue-green and oblong . . ." Yep. ". . . flat or wavy . . ." These are flat. ". . . toothless . . ." Yep. ". . . one to three inches long . . ." Yep. "Acorns are oval to cylindrical, with a rounded tip." I look down at my feet and see dozens of shiny acorns scattered in the duff. I scoop up a handful. Each is oval-shaped with a small rounded tip.

It's definite. I am standing beneath an Engelmann oak. The arboreal equivalent of a Siberian tiger or a black rhino. One of a vanishing species.

I slip the smooth, shiny acorns in my pocket. The Nature Conservancy warns visitors to the Santa Rosa Plateau to stay on marked trails and restrict activities to those "compatible with complex natural communities." I guiltily consider whether absconding with a few acorns will disturb the natural balance. Would I be changing history? The acorns I pocket might otherwise grow into great Engelmann oak leaders.

I note that hundreds more lie at my feet, so I decide to keep a few. They will be souvenirs of my introduction to the Engelmann oak. Plus, an old superstition says that carrying an acorn in your pocket preserves your youthfulness. That sounds like a pleasing alternative to plastic surgery.

I pass another Engelmann oak, its muscular limbs outstretched like arms. In the wispy fog the tree's gray, furrowed bark and towering height give it a fatherly presence. Its stern presence compels me to tread respectfully at its feet.

Reverence for and even outright worship of trees was one of humanity's earliest forms of divine ritual. Trees offered our ancestors an easily understood ideal. Their branches symbolized the heavens, their trunks supported the universe and connected earth and sky. Early societies admired the virtues of trees—their strength and longevity, the sustenance of their fruits, the utility of their wood. But those societies also feared the darkness of the vast forests that enveloped much of the world. Spirits, both good and evil, were thought to inhabit individual trees. Over the centuries, as religious concepts changed, these spirits and gods were freed of the bounds of particular trees and instead came to be associated with entire species.

For the people of Europe and the Near East, the genus that has held more significance than any other is the oak family. The ancient Greeks, and later the Romans, considered oaks to be sacred. The Greeks consecrated the oak to Zeus; the Romans, to Jupiter. These gods were credited with bringing rain to dry Mediterranean lands, and they controlled nature's most spectacular special effect—the thunderbolt. Zeus and Jupiter loved thunder and lightning. They tossed it about with abandon. So did the Norse god Thor. The Norse people dedicated the oak to him and considered the thunderbolt to be Thor's hammer. Many have speculated that oaks came to be associated with the gods of the storm because the oak tends to get struck by lightning more frequently than any other tree—perhaps because oaks grow in isolated locations, such as on hilltops.

The Greeks believed that Zeus announced his will through a live oak that grew at the village of Dodona in Epirus. A holy order of women attended to this most sacred of trees. When a supplicant questioned the oracular oak, a priestess would divine an answer from its rustling leaves. After each communiqué she would announce, "Thus speaks Zeus."

•

The sun starts to burn through the fog blanketing the Santa Rosa Plateau. A chorus of birdcalls greets its warmth. Except for the meadowlark, these birds do not sing the cheery avian melodies I expect. Instead they cluck and bawk. If I didn't know better, I'd think I was in a barnyard. Through the fog I also hear the big *kathump* of distant artillery. The Santa Rosa Plateau is located a few miles from Camp Pendleton. Birds must be adaptable creatures, because their clucks don't miss a beat, even when one of the Marines' 105-millimeter shells explodes and the hills shudder.

As the mists thin, I begin to discern the terrain around me. Gently rolling hills stretch into the distance. Big oaks dot broad, sloping hillsides. Tufts of grass—what biologists call bunchgrass—blanket the plains. Those same scientists often describe this type of habitat as savanna, similar to the vast plains of Africa. It does bear a mild resemblance to the Mara or the Serengeti. From a distance the spreading oaks could be cousins of African acacia trees. I half expect a giraffe to stroll from behind one.

My trail climbs a hill covered with a thicket of shrub oak. The top branches of these miniature oaks weave together overhead, enclosing a tunnel six feet high. Coating every branch in this miniature forest is thick, scaly lichen the color of key lime pie.

The tunnel seems like it would make a good photograph, so I pause to snap it. Recently I bought a camera to illustrate my walking expeditions. But now when I hike, I spend lots of time considering what constitutes a good picture. Those brainwaves seem to be crowding out the internal monologue that normally fills my mind when I'm on the trail. One of the main attractions of my small journeys around Los Angeles has been the opportunity to engage in some serious thinking. Composing a good picture rarely seems as valuable as composing a good thought. (Assuming, of course, that you're not an Ansel Adams.) As I emerge from the shrub oaks and surmount a hilltop, I see, superimposed against the fog, an old oak—its huge trunk grown into the shape of a Y. Does this sight prod me to philosophize? No. Instead I think, Ah, this would make a good picture.

As I approach this distinguished Engelmann oak, I spot a good-sized knothole and peer into it. Split trunks and holes left from broken limbs are common in old oaks. Mature oaks often become so gnarled that their tortured appearance has prompted many cultures to suspect them of being haunted. In *The Tempest,* the magician Prospero warns his sprightly servant Ariel that

> If thou more murmur'st, I will rend an oak,
> And peg thee in his knotty entrails, till
> Thou hast howl'd away twelve winters.

Through the centuries many cultures have believed that the cracks and holes in oaks serve as portals to other worlds. Some Europeans thought elves inhabited hollow oaks. An old English saying held that the elves fly away in autumn on the brown oak leaves.

In this hole I see no elves. That is probably just as well. Humans should interact with such magical creatures at their own risk. In Wales a story tells of fairies (close cousins of elves, in British legends) who enchanted a young man sitting under a tree. He thought he was listening to the song of a bird. After what seemed a few minutes, the song ended. The young man looked up and saw that the tree above him was withered and dead. When he returned home, his house looked different, and a strange old man was living there. He questioned the man, and discovered him to be his own grandnephew! The young man had lain under the tree for three generations and was not released from the fairies' spell until the last of the tree's sap had dried. When the grandnephew hugged him, the young man crumbled into dust.

I turn up the collar on my shirt. Folk wisdom says this gesture protects you when passing through country haunted by elves.

Fear of elves and their spells did not stop King Charles II from hiding in the split trunk of an oak after his army of Scotsmen suffered defeat at the battle of Worcester in 1651. As a result he evaded capture by Oliver Cromwell's forces. When he was later restored to the throne, Charles declared May 29 to be Royal Oak Day, also known as Oak Apple Day. (An oak apple is a tumorous growth, called a gall, that can develop into many fantastic shapes, such as stars, cups, and crowns, though most resemble apples. Galls form on oaks when certain types of wasps deposit their eggs in the tree's bark.) The English celebrated Oak Apple Day by wearing gilded oak galls on their clothing, adorning their hats with oak leaves, hanging oak branches over their doors, and general rejoicing.

Besides the knothole in the old Y-shaped oak, many other smaller holes perforate its bark. They're all an inch deep and the diameter of a nickel—too small, I suspect, for elves. Acorn woodpeckers drill these holes into oaks, telephone poles, fence posts, and any other convenient slab of wood. During the autumn this industrious species gathers acorns and caches them in the holes it has chiseled, later removing the acorns and eating them during bad weather and the spring breeding season. Generations of acorn woodpeckers will maintain a single storage site, known as a granary. Up in the treetops I hear an *arack arack,* which I believe is the call of the acorn woodpecker. Or an elf.

I fidget with my collar and march on.

When I pass a pole-sized oak sapling, I stop to inspect it. The leaves of this young tree have teeth, indicating it is not an Engelmann. By consulting my guidebook, I confirm that this is not *Quercus engelmannii* but *Quercus agrifolia,* or the coast live oak, another species common on the Santa Rosa Plateau. This disappoints me a bit because today I hope to find a younger generation of Engelmann oaks. Coast live oaks are not endangered, and it is not uncommon to find young ones at this point in their development, a phase biologists call the "recruitment" stage—when saplings make the transition to pole-sized trees.

Several species of California oaks are not recruiting. The ecologist James R. Griffin was one of the first scientists to raise the alarm over this phenomenon. In 1971 he wrote in *Fremontia,* the journal of the California Native Plant Society, "Where are the young trees under the big oaks? At first glance there seems to be none. One can drive through literally tens of thousands of acres and not see a single Valley Oak sapling."

The Engelmann is another oak species experiencing this same sad fate. Its plight reminds me of a tale from *The Lord of the Rings,* Tolkien's masterpiece of fantasy, involving Ents— creatures who are fourteen feet tall and clad in bark. The Ents are tree shepherds and closely resemble the trees they herd. A melancholy had taken hold of Tolkien's Ents because, as one said, "There have been no Entings—no children, you would say, for a terrible long count of years. You see, we lost the Entwives." One by one the Ents were falling asleep and turning into members of their own flock.

Similarly, for the Engelmann oaks few Engelmannings have appeared for a terrible long count of years. Perhaps they have lost their Engelmannwives. Or we humans have driven them off.

I start walking up a long, gentle, grassy slope. At the crest of this rise stands a solitary oak. I decide I will rest when I reach its shade.

The fog is clearing, and as I climb I feel the heat of the day for the first time. At the summit, I follow a little path off the main trail to the circle of earth sheltered by the lone Engelmann. The tree's huge limbs reach out twenty feet or more in all directions until they arch back down to the ground. Several hundred people could sit comfortably beneath this oak. Its canopy forms a hemisphere of deep shade and bird song.

Near the town of Chico in the Sacramento Valley, settlers of California discovered an oak so large that on a summer day it could shade *nine thousand people.* Its canopy was one hundred fifty feet across, its trunk more than nine feet wide. This titanic tree was named the Hooker Oak, after the British botanist Joseph Hooker. In 1877 Hooker traveled from England to California to inspect this remarkable specimen; in 1977 the great Hooker Oak fell, a victim of old age.

America can boast of many other historic oaks. Aaron Burr was tried for treason under the shade of one. Davy Crockett and George Armstrong Custer each camped beneath oaken boughs on the way to their respective dates with destiny. For more than a decade during the 1800s, an oak near Council Grove, Kansas, was the only post office box for hundreds of miles along the Santa Fe Trail.

The leafy canopy of a California oak is a well-designed machine for capturing sunlight. The outer leaves of the tree are small, waxy, and loaded with photosynthetic cells that can harness sunlight to generate carbohydrates. The small size of the leaves allows excess heat to dissipate. Their waxy coating prevents the semi-arid climate from sucking precious moisture out of the tree. Farther inside the canopy the leaves are larger, the better to catch any stray light rays that have penetrated the outer shell of leaves. The limbs of the oak twist and turn, growing as much horizontally as vertically, which enables the tree to reach for the maximum amount of sunlight and pack as many leaves as possible onto each branch.

This oak's drooping, serpentine limbs seem to call out for someone to scale its green heights. I consider it, but decide to stay earthbound. Tree climbing might not be "compatible with a complex natural community."

From this hilltop oak, the trail strikes out across a shallow grassy bowl a half-mile wide. Not a single tree grows in this expanse. At the base of the bowl, a patch of reeds forms a dark outline in the grass; the shoots are still wet with dew while the rest of the hillside is already bone dry. This lowland holds moisture longer than the well-drained hillsides. Perched on the reeds, an exaltation of meadowlarks lets loose a lilting chorus. Their song blends nicely with the distant spattering of heavy machine guns.

On the far side of this grassy bowl the vegetation looks ragged. Although the Santa Rosa Plateau has been a Nature Conservancy Reserve for nine years, that hillside has the distinctive look of overgrazing. As I near it, I see why. Barbed wire marks the reserve's boundary. Beyond that a herd of Big Macs (still in their quaint four-legged phase) munch on sparse tufts of grass. The quality of vegetation on either side of the fence forms a stark contrast. Even on this December day, after seven straight months of dry weather, the grasses on the Conservancy side are sere but otherwise abundant and healthy. On the rancher's side spindly tufts dot a field of bare dirt. Some might claim that's the price we pay if we want prime rib for dinner. I say, Eat more rice and beans.

On my side of the fence, rusting barbed wire lies coiled on the ground. This wire must have marked a property line until the Nature Conservancy bought the land. Now fence posts have been pulled up and strewn about. To see barbed wire unstrung—the land being freed of its shackles—is a joyful thing.

The trail soon leads me into another dim oak woodland. Robert Louis Stevenson described the live oak forests of California as "woods for murderers to crawl around in." He was right. Here the trees brood. Their limbs are gray or splashed green with lichen. They writhe and contort; branches seem to grasp for me. No wonder our ancestors imagined that twisted trees harbored malicious spirits. The peasants of Devonshire used to believe that the spirits of the forest would lead travelers astray into ditches and bogs, especially at night. They called this being "pixie-led." The pixies—another close relative of elves—would sit in the trees and laugh at the poor soul's plight.

Aside from slight anxieties about elves, fairies, and pixies, I walk today with a clear mind. The Santa Rosa Plateau Ecological Reserve abuts the eastern slope of the Santa Ana Mountains, home to thirty or more mountain lions. Although the common scientific wisdom maintains that mountain lions are incredibly reclusive, the news media—and maybe the lions themselves—are working to dispel this notion. In the last three years mountain lions have slain three unfortunate Americans, and several years ago they twice attacked children just a few miles from the fields where I now walk. Crossing these grassy, open plains today, however, I find it hard to fret about instant death at the hands (or teeth) of large predators. Maybe the song of meadowlarks soothes my anxieties.

The only other large predator that may pass this way is a bear. Before the Spaniards arrived in California, the grizzly bear was widespread in oak country like this. Acorns were a major source of food for *Ursus horribilis,* and the sight of grizzlies feeding under California oaks was a common one to both Indians and white settlers. Early observers reported that the grizzlies would throw themselves upon an oak limb that held acorns and swing on it until the limb broke, sending branch, acorns, and bear crashing to the ground. Younger grizzlies would climb trees and break off branches, tossing them down to adults on the ground. The western poet Joaquin Miller wrote that he had seen grizzlies "feeding under the oaks in Napa Valley in numbers together . . . as composedly and as careless of danger as if they had been hogs feeding on nuts under the hickory trees of the Wabash."

I'd dearly love to watch a grizzly swatting at one of these Engelmann oaks. From a good safe distance, of course. Grizzlies probably should have been more cautious about the danger posed by the European colonists, because they exterminated the bears within 150 years. So much for the symbol of California. That image on the state flag might just as well be a unicorn.

There is a remote chance I could see a black bear today. Although they are not native to Southern California, in 1933 rangers from Yosemite National Park relocated twenty-seven overly spirited bears to the San Gabriel and San Bernardino Mountains around Los Angeles. There they prospered, and now bears abound in the mountains around LA. Black bears have been spotted as far south as Orange and San Diego counties—50 to 150 miles away from the San Gabriel Range. Experts dismiss these reports, pointing out how many free-

ways and other human barriers a bear would have to surmount to migrate that far south. Yet in 1992 a motorist killed
a black bear in northern San Diego County. Wildlife officials
claim a human had released the creature into the wild.

In general I find it hard to worry about any kind of mortal
danger when the terrain I'm crossing looks like the Sheep
Meadow in New York's Central Park. If a dangerous creature
such as a bear, mountain lion, or street gang member were
approaching, I could see the menace a mile away. Many
psychologists and biologists, including E. O. Wilson, the
noted Harvard expert on biodiversity, have postulated that
my peace of mind and the land's resemblance to Central Park
are linked phenomena.

When people around the world are given the opportunity
to choose where they live, they generally select open, tree-
studded land on prominences overlooking water. Those individuals and organizations with the most money and power
frequently place their castles or seats of government or corporate headquarters on heights of land amid scattered trees
overlooking water. When people are crowded into urban
landscapes or featureless terrain, they labor to recreate open
landscapes dotted with large spreading trees. Ancient Romans built gardens with well-spaced, spreading trees. So did
the Japanese and Chinese. And the British gentry. And Frederick Law Olmsted in Central Park. And millions of Americans when they fled our urban centers to settle suburbia. The
landscapes these disparate peoples have created all bear a no-
ticeable resemblance to African savanna.

As the Europeans colonized North America, they had the
opportunity to settle many types of habitat. Their preferred
choice was not dark, looming forest, barren desert, or
swampy bayou. When given a chance, they opted for open
terrain broken occasionally by trees and preferably overlook-

ing water. If they could not find that sort of landscape, they reproduced it—with great effort. Two hundred years ago, settlers cleared the great forests of the northeastern United States, leaving behind open country with scattered trees. In North America we are still generating these kinds of habitats. Just look at the newest housing developments outside Las Vegas: open, tree-studded, parklike lands encircle manmade lakes—in the middle of the parched Nevada desert.

This convergence of human activities may be a large coincidence, but Wilson suggests a far more fundamental explanation. We like those kind of locales, he says, "for the same general reason that sugar is sweet." Innate human responses have a particular meaning rooted in our species' past. Tastes in food, mating habits, social patterns, and our clear preference for certain types of environments are no exception. *Homo erectus,* the predecessor to *Homo sapiens,* evolved on the savannas of Africa. For two million years, those abundant plains provided our ancestors with plenty of food and game. Clumps of trees, particularly acacias, sheltered *H. erectus* from sun, wind, and rain. The long views across the savannas afforded them plenty of warning when predatory animals or rival bands of proto-humans approached. It was an excellent environment for omnivorous bipeds.

Thus, our species' preference for open terrain amid well-spaced trees is not just an emotional reaction; it is an evolutionary response that has been genetically programmed into our thinking and reflected in our likes and dislikes over two million years.

And I thought I just liked big trees.

•

I pass what my trail map calls a vernal pool—poorly drained terrain that floods in the spring and dries out during the summer. This particular vernal pool looks like a baked mud puddle. Only recently recognized as an important type of wetland, vernal pools in dry California country like this support many rare life forms, such as the endangered fairy shrimp, which lays its eggs in the spring when water floods the pool. These tiny crustaceans die as the pool evaporates, but their eggs lodge in cracks in the mud, then hatch when rain fills the pool the following winter.

At my feet on the trail I spot a device so fiendish it's hard to believe it is a creation of Nature and not some mad engineer. It is the fruit of *Erodium cicutarium,* a plant commonly known as a storksbill. The fruit is shaped like a thick needle; some people think it resembles the bill of a stork. As it dries, seeds from the storksbill peel away in strands and spiral into the shape of a corkscrew. The base of the seed forms a right angle to the direction of the screw; it makes an effective handle. The screw of the *Erodium* easily snags a ride on anything that passes. Like a pair of socks. Or a dog's ear. Touch the handle and the screw bores in deeper. The storksbill is a Mediterranean native. It probably traveled to the New World in the pantaloons of some conquistador. I slip the storksbill in my pocket. Later I will dispose of it properly. When I find a vat of acid.

When I reach for the storksbill, a grasshopper springs away from my approaching hand. I widen the focus of my eyes and see hoppers everywhere. As the sun warms the field, they come to life, lazily springing between clumps of grass.

In the last few years an infestation of grasshoppers has struck this region, ravaging the leaves of oak seedlings and straining their ability to recruit. This insect plague, however, is merely one of the myriad problems that the Engelmann oaks confront. The full range of assaults on their viability exemplifies what the word *ecology* originally meant, before it became a pop-culture synonym for environmental concern. Ecology is the study of relationships between organisms and their environment.

One type of organism threatening the existence of the Engelmann oak is the cow. On grazing lands like those I saw beyond the barbed wire, the hooves of livestock compact soil, making it difficult for acorns to take root. Cattle and sheep munch acorns, reducing the number of seeds that can possibly germinate, and they also graze on the leaves and branches of any oak seedlings that do sprout.

Wild creatures also feed on Engelmann oaks. Deer eat up to three hundred acorns a day, and they too graze on the leaves and branches of seedlings and young trees. The deer population typically increases when large predators, such as mountain lions, become scarce. Pocket gophers, mice, and ground squirrels also dine voraciously on acorns and the roots of young trees, and their numbers similarly multiply when populations of smaller predators, like bobcats and foxes, decline.

Probably the biggest and most intractable threat to the survival of the Engelmann oak is the spread of nonnative grasses and weeds. These plants form dense blankets of vegetation that grow more rapidly in the spring than do native flora, thus winning the competition for nutrients and water. Brushfires normally offer oaks a second chance for survival by stripping the land clean of all vegetation. After a wildfire, oak seedlings can shoot up fast, allowing them to capture sunlight from their shorter neighbors. Periodic burning was a common practice among the Indians, but today many Californians don't feel comfortable torching land that adjoins their half-million-dollar dream homes.

As E. O. Wilson says, "Everything matters in some unseen but vital way." The mountain lions, the pocket gophers, the fairy shrimp. The Engelmann oaks matter too; but evidently, we do not appreciate their value yet, because we are letting them slip away. We are violating the first rule of the tinkerer, according to the influential ecologist and writer Aldo Leopold: Don't throw away any of the parts.

•

The trail now swings across a field blanketed with a jumble of small gray rocks. Rising up from between the stones is a small stand of young Engelmann oaks. At last. I pick my way across the meadow toward the recruits and inspect six young trees, four with trunks two inches across and another couple three inches wide. Either the Engelmannwives have visited here or something about this rocky terrain nurtures young oaks.

The average oak produces six to seven thousand acorns a year, and one study estimates that if only one acorn *in a million* survives each year, a forest could replace itself. Yet the Engelmanns are not achieving even that paltry rate.

Trees are patient. They can tolerate disruptions in their reproductive cycle wreaked upon them by man and Nature. Although some Engelmanns survive 300 to 400 years, most live only about 150. So the Engelmann oak can wait 50 years to reproduce, maybe even 100. But it can't wait forever.

In 150 years, when most of the mature Engelmann oaks on the Santa Rosa Plateau have been reduced to dust, these six trees in front of me may be the last of their species.

"Boys," I announce to the recruits, "there's a lot riding on you."

•

I cross the brow of a ridge and ahead see a sweeping expanse of undulating grassy hills, dotted with clumps of trees. In the distance bigger hills rise into the haze. It's beautiful, peaceful country. Makes me want to homestead.

Just kidding. Those ancient feelings—I have to quash them. Southern California has absorbed enough homesteaders. There's fifteen million of us sodbusters here in the Los Angeles Standard Metropolitan Statistical Area. In the expanse I survey, however, I see not a single human. Nor a cow. Nor a sheep. And that's exactly the way this land should remain.

As I descend into the broad valley, I flush a large raptor from its perch on a tree thirty yards away. Staying behind the cover of several trees, the big golden-colored bird flaps away. I scramble to pull binoculars from my pack. Too late. By the time I have enhanced my vision, the big bird has cleared the next ridgeline. I still have never definitively seen a golden eagle in the wild.

I decide to strap my binoculars to my belt, but that makes me feel rather ridiculous. In addition to them, I now dangle a camera from my neck because I don't trust my memory to see; I wear a hat to shield myself from the harsh rays of the sun; I carry a walking stick to improve my balance; and I pack food, water, and extra clothing, because I can't survive in Nature for very long without any of them. What pathetic creatures we humans are. (Pathetic? Ha! Give me a bulldozer and a few gallons of diesel. I'll show Nature a thing or two.)

I see some acorn woodpeckers swooping between two big Engelmanns, and I carefully stalk beneath those trees. The woodpeckers flee my scrutiny, but my curiosity is rewarded with the discovery of a good-sized active woodpecker granary. The limbs of these oaks are riddled with holes, most of them filled with acorns. In the background I hear the woodpecker's *arack, arack.*

I'm not sure how these clever birds insert their acorns into some of these holes, the fit is so tight. Maybe they have placed nuts there in previous years and the wood has healed around them. I'm glad to see these birds are thinking ahead, saving for the future, remembering that their kids may want to go to Woodpecker U and they'll need plenty of acorns. They differ in this respect from most Americans.

The highly nutritious acorns produced by California oaks formed the foundation for many Native American cultures. They were to the Indians of California what bison were to the tribes of the Great Plains and corn was to the Indian nations of the Southwest. A family of California Indians could gather up to 140 pounds of acorns in a day, 20 percent of their annual needs. The Indians of California conducted many ceremonies and rituals to ensure good harvests. When one tribe attempted to usurp another's acorn supply, they sometimes fought wars. California Indians often invoked oaks as symbols of life and fertility. The Wintu tribe would tie the umbilical cord of a newborn boy to the limb of an oak to ensure that the child grew up alert and bold. Presumably the umbilical had already fallen off.

European cultures held the oak in equally high esteem. The Celts of pre-Christian Europe, and their priestly class, the Druids, venerated the oak like no other people before or since. In fact, some etymologists believe the word *druid* means "men of oak." In that era in Germany, peeling the bark off any standing tree warranted a fierce punishment. The offender's navel was cut out and nailed to the part of the tree that had been wounded. Then the offender was forced to circle the tree, unraveling his intestines to bind the tree's wound. (A punishment that matched the crime, if ever there was one.) In pagan Europe marriages were often conducted under oaks, and in the ensuing Christian days newly married couples covered all bases by hurrying from the church after their vows and dancing around an oak tree. During trials in thirteenth-century France, litigants were made to stand under an oak.

The first to be touched by a fallen leaf was deemed innocent. In more recent times, bobbins in the shape of acorns were attached to the cords that raise window blinds. The acorn was believed to prevent lightning from striking the house. Young lovers used to drop two acorns in a bowl of water. If the nuts floated together, the couple would be united in marriage.

•

Out in the open grasslands animal trails branch across the hills. The grass on each path is partially trampled, enough that the trail is clearly marked but not so much that the plant dies. These animal byways etch the landscape like capillaries.

A gust of wind whispers past my ear and sends a wave rippling across the savanna. When the peasants of Burgundy and Neuchâtel saw swirls pass like that through fields of corn, they whispered that the Green Lady was afoot. Yet another malicious denizen of the wilds, the Green Lady was fond of stripping a man of his possessions and dragging him through the briars.

The trail loops through the grasslands and down toward the base of the broad valley. Here I am sheltered from all sounds of humanity. No distant traffic noise. No machine guns. Just the wind rustling through the grass and the oaks. That sound was said to have inspired Japhet, the son of Noah, to invent the first musical instrument. For the ancient Greeks the song of the sighing wind was the sound of a harp played by Aeolus, King of the Winds.

Thus spoke Zeus's great-great-great-grandson.

At the base of the broad valley, my trail joins a dirt road that swings past an old adobe. The building is typical of Spanish colonial architecture in California—a small one-story structure with a front porch running the full length of the house. Beyond the adobe sits a trailer that serves as the headquarters for the Nature Conservancy staff—typical architecture of late-twentieth-century America.

I walk around the adobe, peer in its windows, see no one. The only mammalians present today besides me are a few ground squirrels dashing around a woodpile.

Next to the adobe sits a large gray boulder. A plaque is mounted to it. The inscription reads "Rancho Santa Rosa. 47,815.1 acres granted by Governor Pio Pico to Juan Moreno, January 30, 1846 and patented to him by the United States, October 10, 1872."

Old Juan's homestead is sheltered by several monster oaks. One must be hundreds of years old. Doubtless it was full grown when this adobe was built. Nearby sway some willows, their leaves a golden yellow at this time of year, a few eucalyptus, and, God forbid, some palm trees.

The wind gusts through the big oaks. The Aeolian harp. That's good. Makes eternal music. And keeps the gnats down.

As I leave the adobe, I see a yellow truck bouncing down the road toward me. Thinking it must be a Nature Conservancy staffer, I pause. But it parks in front of some Port-o-Potties. The logo on the side of the truck reads "Right Way Portable Toilets." I wave to the driver as he makes his appointed rounds.

•

The trail winds into a valley where the hillsides are covered with chaparral, and here I smell something so fragrant it stops me in my tracks. I start sniffing like a hound and soon determine the source of this heavenly aroma to be a clump of sagebrush. Its pungent odor mixes with the smell of decomposing leaves and wet earth. Fantastic! Chanel couldn't bottle a better scent.

The brush thickens. Lining the trail are many of my old

friends from other hikes through chaparral—ceanothus, chamise, toyon. But by far the most common form of vegetation here is shrub oak. The word *chaparral* derives from the Spanish *chaparro,* for evergreen oak. Spanish settlers applied the term to stands of evergreen shrub oak that blanket hillsides throughout Southern California.

In some spots along the trail, shrub oak and chamise loom five feet higher than my head. This trail feels wilder than other paths in the reserve. Here there's an edge. Danger could lurk a few feet away. The broad vistas elsewhere evoke a peaceful, civilized quality—thanks to that mile of warning the open grasslands offer should a predator or a proto-human be approaching. In this dense chaparral, however, when I pass a few oaks rising above the brush and see the circles of earth their deep shade leaves clear, I let out a little hurrah. The pioneers are clearing the land.

The trail descends a little valley, crosses a creek, and climbs up until it reaches the edge of the savanna. Again my line of sight leaps out for miles, and my spirits lift a commensurate amount. The lunch whistle goes off. I stop in the dappled sunlight beneath a great coast live oak and lean my walking stick against a knothole in its trunk. Then I pause. Who's inside that hole? Should I risk a three-generation nap? Pamela is expecting me for dinner.

Taking the chance, I turn up my collar and sit at the edge of the path. I rummage through my pack for lunch. After five hours on the trail, that peanut butter and jelly sandwich tastes like ambrosia.

I pick an acorn from the duff around me and study its shiny surface. Cracking it open, I nibble at the nut. The meat is so bitter it almost turns my mouth inside out.

Unlike cows, sheep, deer, bears, and woodpeckers, humans perceive the taste of raw acorns to be bitter. This is because acorns contain tannin. The Indians of California who relied on acorns for their diet pulverized them into flour and then filtered the meal with water to leach out the tannin. Once purified, the acorn meal could be cooked as mush or baked into a bread that turned naturally sweet. John Muir declared acorn bread to be the most nutritious food he ever ate. He often carried dried loaves during his lengthy explorations of California.

Acorns and the rest of the oak have been put to many other uses over the centuries. American pioneers sometimes added acorn flour to their brewing vats to give beers a distinctive nutty flavor. Oak leaves were fermented to make wine. Oak tannin was used for curing leather. (Thus the word *tanning*.) Acorns were even used for making coffee. A nineteenth-century housekeeping book claimed acorn coffee was good for curing "slimy obstructions of the viscera."

Before I leave my resting place, I study the trunk of the big coast live oak standing before me, looking for a creature called the arboreal salamander. This type of salamander is lungless; it absorbs oxygen directly through the skin. To survive the dry California summer, the arboreal salamander finds a crevice, often in the bark of a live oak, and estivates—that is, it spends the hot months in a stupor. (I spent a few summers like that in Philadelphia.) When the rains arrive in winter, the arboreal salamander returns to life by soaking up water for hours until it is rehydrated.

According to a legend that Greek woodcutters have handed down, a live oak was used to make Christ's cross. The tale holds that when Jesus was to be crucified, the trees of the forest held a council and decided they would not allow their wood to be used for such an evil purpose. When woodcutters came to take timber for the crucifixion, they swung their axes at many trees and every one split itself into useless fragments—except one, the live oak. For centuries Greek woodcutters treated the live oak as a pariah, a second Judas.

•

After lunch my trail winds back out across the savanna. Meadowlarks perch on any high spot they can find in the grass. Their yellow breasts shine like fireflies; their songs sound like angels.

On a grassy hillside I spot some white objects strewn across fifty yards of turf. These mysterious white things lie well off the trail, and I don't want to violate the Nature Conservancy's rules, so I pull out my binoculars to examine them. The white objects are bones. Big leg bones, sections of vertebrae, broken ribs. They look like they're from either a cow or a deer. The Great Wheel of Life spins on.

My trail intersects a dirt road and, after consulting the map, I determine I must follow this dusty lane. It climbs a steep hill, and the quality of the walking deteriorates drastically. Deep ruts furrow the road, and jumbles of small rocks render the footing shaky. The grass beside the road looks distressed, probably from cattle grazing. Scattered around is an even more reliable indicator of bovine visitors—old cow pies.

Soon a trail that is not marked on my map angles away from the road and traverses the face of the hill, forming an inviting curve through more luxuriant grass. A road, I decide, performs the mundane task of getting from point A to point B. A trail is for enjoying yourself along the way. Not knowing where this path will take me, I invoke the spirit of Robert Frost and follow it.

I pass some deer scat, stained brick orange and sprinkled

with acorn shells. Good for curing slimy obstructions of the viscera.

Soon I roust a coyote. He springs up out of the grass twenty yards away and scampers off, then ensconces himself on a hillside seventy yards distant to inspect me. When I stop, he gives ground, cautiously glancing back at me, no doubt thinking, "What the hell is a *human* doing out here on a *Thursday?*" Clever doggie. Coyotes haven't overcome the destruction mankind has rained on them and in the process extended their range *all the way to Maine* by acting dumb.

The trail soon leads down into flat terrain broken by solitary, elephantine rocks and scattered, parklike stands of oaks. The Nature Conservancy has performed some controlled burns in this area. (I've always believed there's no problem so big that you can't set it right with a flamethrower.) Fresh clumps of grass poke up through blackened stalks. Most of the oaks here seem to have shrugged off the flame. Engelmanns have thick bark that insulates them from brief episodes of fire. Dormant buds on their branches quickly sprout to replace any smaller limbs that burn during fast-moving wildfires.

I wander into a grove of huge unscathed oaks clustered around a circle of gray boulders. The wind gusts up. Perhaps I have heard too much Aeolian music by this time, because this grove immediately strikes me as having a mystical aura. I sense a wisdom in this circle of rocks and trees.

The Druids forbade the building of temples or the worship of gods within walls and under roofs. They placed their holy sites in the deepest recesses of the forest and planted groves of trees to mark these spots. Their preferred tree for sacred sites was the oak. In the center of a holy grove they typically also erected a circle of stones. Many of the ancient Christian churches across northern Europe were built on the sites of these Druid holy places. Some of those first churches had no roofs, consistent with Druid creed.

Walking between the rocks of the First Druid Church of the Santa Rosa Plateau, I sink into a drift of oak leaves as if they were a deep snowbank. I flail for a second, then dive for firmer footing onto a nearby boulder. Perhaps the Druid priests don't like having an infidel trudging across their hallowed ground.

I stretch out on the big gray rock and lie still, trying to understand the wisdom of the rustling leaves. Because the ancients believed trees spoke wisdom, they wore crowns of leaves, the better to hear the knowledge of the whispering woods.

Trying to tune in Zeus, I press a few oak leaves to my head. Nothing.

I usually maintain a healthy skepticism toward mystical thinking, but when I lie at the foot of these Engelmann oaks, I easily succumb. These trees grab my imagination as if it had handlebars. Perhaps that is the value of these oaks. *Everything matters in some unseen but vital way.*

Someday accountants may be able to enter the value of the Engelmann oak onto their spreadsheets. Perhaps plant geneticists will splice the genomes of the Engelmann oak with potato chromosomes so that russets can be cultivated in the tropical summer of Idaho after the greenhouse effect really kicks in. One day medical researchers may use the oak's amino acids to form a compound that will arrest drug-resistant pneumonia. But undoubtedly the value of many species will remain less quantifiable.

Perhaps the vital function of the Engelmann oak is, simply, to act like an oak. This tree—and all of the other members of its genus—have firmly grasped the human imagination for thousands of years. Oaks offer a doorway to some kinds of thinking that we humans used to take for granted but lost somewhere along the centuries. Once oaks formed the basis of a major religion. Perhaps one day they will inspire another.

Allowing the Engelmann oak, or any species for that matter, to fall off the ark is an act that humanity should not permit without grave consideration. *The first rule of the tinkerer is to keep all the pieces.*

●

I start the last leg of my hike. The shadows are lengthening. It's only three o'clock, but the sun never rises high on late December days. I keep expecting to find a trail marker or a road that leads back to the entrance of the reserve. None appears. After walking a half hour, I discover barbed wire blocking my advance. Not too far beyond the fence I can see the highway that borders the edge of the reserve. But my car is not in sight.

After studying my low-resolution trail map, I conclude that I am about a mile from the entrance where I parked. Evidently following the road less traveled has gotten me a little lost. Not completely lost, mind you, because I could climb this fence, head straight for the highway, and follow it back to the car. But after an exceptionally pleasant day of traipsing through woods and meadows, tromping down a hard, smelly asphalt road would assault my sensitivities. Alternatively, I could bushwhack straight to where I believe the main gate of the reserve is located. But leaving the trail would violate the Conservancy's rules. The Vibram soles on my boots would be performing an act "incompatible with a complex natural community."

I see another hiker in the distance. Damn. After seven hours, I was beginning to think these hills were reserved exclusively for me—and the Right Way Sanitary Service man.

I could hail this fellow and ask him for directions, but to do so less than a half-mile from the road would be humiliating.

Instead I cast about on my own for the correct trail. Many present themselves. None are marked with a familiar name— or any name at all. I pick one. After hoofing it a long way up and down several hills, it leads me back to the same barbed-wire barrier.

I backtrack.

Taking another trail that seems to lead in the appropriate direction, I soon confront a sign: Area closed for habitat restoration.

I backtrack.

The shadows grow long. Only one and a half more hours of daylight. A chill creeps into the air, and I roll down my sleeves.

I pass an old oak. The knots and curves on its trunk seem to have frozen into a frowning face. If ever a tree had someone pegged in its knotty entrails, this is it. After I pass, I glance back to make sure this grim old tree spirit isn't laughing at me. Its features seem immobile, though I thought I heard a faint "harrumph."

The trail finally peters out on the banks of a small but deep creek. Very good year-round habitat for amphibians. Very bad for humans who like dry feet. I'd need hip boots to wade this stream.

I stare in the direction that seems to head back toward the car. Another sign: Area closed.

An hour of light remaining. I turn back.

I'm starting to feel pixie-led. Is that a chuckle I hear in the treetops?

I turn up the collar on my shirt.

Then, across a wide field I see the glint of sun on a windshield. My car. And a trail, albeit a faint one, cuts straight for it.

I tiptoe across the fragile habitat.

With my passage home assured, I take one last break, sit on a boulder, and eat a crisp, sweet apple. The sun is low; the savanna shimmers in golden light. The scattered oaks look almost purple. I watch the Green Lady ripple over the hillsides. The woodpeckers are *arack aracking*. The meadowlarks warble.

Reaching for my keys, I find the acorns that I pocketed when I encountered my first Engelmann oak this morning.

I slip one back into my pocket. Perhaps when all the Engelmann oaks are gone, I will hold this last precious seed, this shiny reservoir of genetic information. I will be the guardian of this repository of oak-ness.

For the remainder, however, I have a plan.

I look around for Nature Conservancy officials and see none. Surreptitiously, I take the acorns and drop them into crevices around the boulder on which I sit. With my walking stick, I fill the cracks with dirt.

I beg the pardon of the Nature Conservancy for mucking around with the balance of life. Unfortunately I don't think we can wait for the return of the Engelmannwives. No magical beings are stepping forward to act as stewards on our ark. It's up to you and me. Only we have the power to ensure that all our passengers survive the voyage.

Thus speaks Zeus.

Lie Down with Lions

. . . . . .

Some years ago, Susan Mattern-Small and her husband Donald Small took a Sunday afternoon hike in Ronald W. Caspers Wilderness Park, a preserve in Orange County, California. They brought David, their nine-year-old son, and Laura, their five-year-old daughter. The Smalls often visited this 7,500-acre park in the foothills of the Santa Ana Mountains. For them and thousands of other Californians, the woods and chaparral in Caspers Park provided an island of natural serenity in the midst of Orange County's thickening urban sprawl.

This particular Sunday in March, the Small family strolled along a nature trail paralleling Bell Creek, a stream that tumbles down from a remote gorge high in the Santa Anas. While Donald and David walked ahead under the oaks and sycamores, Susan and Laura lingered behind. They were wading through the shallows of Bell Creek searching for tadpoles. Laura grew tired of the hunt and climbed up the creek's bank into a small clearing. She heard a rustling. An animal leapt from the bushes. Laura thought it was a big dog.

When Laura's mother turned, she saw a muscular, buff-colored animal seize her daughter's head in its jaws and drag the child away.

At first Susan had the same thought as her daughter. It was a large dog.

In fact, it was a mountain lion.

Susan screamed.

Donald Small and his son heard the scream and ran back to Susan. While David raced for help, Donald and Susan crashed through cacti and tangled brush looking for Laura. Susan heard crying, followed the noise, and stumbled upon the mountain lion. It still held Laura by her head.

Gregory Ysais was hiking nearby when he heard Susan's cries for help. Running toward her, the thirty-six-year-old man from Mission Viejo found Susan and the mountain lion. He tore a branch from a tree and beat the lion away from Laura. Susan rushed to her daughter, gathered the little girl in her arms, and dashed away. Laura's face was torn to pieces; her skull was crushed. Susan thought her daughter might be dead.

Luckily, Susan found a park ranger patrolling the area. The ranger administered first aid and radioed for help. Laura was still alive. Soon the little girl was airlifted by paramedic helicopter to a local hospital.

State wildlife officials called the event unprecedented, the first mountain lion attack on a Californian in over seventy-five years. They closed the park and unleashed trained dogs to track the cat. The next day the dogs treed a small, healthy male mountain lion, less than two years old. After unsuccessfully trying to tranquilize it, the wildlife officers shot and killed the lion.

Miraculously, Laura Small survived her ordeal—although she paid a terrible price. The blond, blue-eyed girl was blinded on one side, and her right arm and leg were partially paralyzed. For years Laura had to wear a bicycle helmet to protect a portion of her brain that was exposed when the cat smashed her skull. Eventually, a plastic plate was implanted in her head to cover the hole, one of fifteen operations she endured over the next six years.

Three months later the Smalls filed lawsuits seeking $28 million in damages from Orange County and the State of California. The Smalls contended that county and state wildlife officials knew mountain lions were frequenting the area but had failed to inform the public of the dangers posed by the big cats. Furthermore, the Smalls charged, park officials had, in effect, lured mountain lions into contact with humans by their placement of watering troughs, which attracted deer, the principal prey of lions.

In October that same year, Timothy Mellon, his wife, and their six-year-old son Justin were hiking in the same part of Caspers Park with a group of ten adults and children. Justin fell behind when he stopped to tie his shoe. As he ran to catch up, a mountain lion sprang on him. One of the other children saw the attack and screamed.

Timothy Mellon heard the scream, ran for his son, and found a mountain lion trying to drag the boy away. The cat had seized Justin by the head. The boy was fighting for his life. Timothy ran at the lion with a small hunting knife, and the animal released the child.

Timothy picked Justin up and handed him to his mother. The lion appeared to be ready to attack again, so once more Timothy brandished the knife. The lion stalked back and forth. Another of Timothy's male companions joined him, and the two men shouted and waved their arms at the lion, trying to hold it at bay while Justin's mother, holding her boy in her arms, ran back down the trail.

The Mellons escaped to safety. Justin required more than a hundred stitches to close up cuts over his entire body.

The next day trackers, game wardens, park rangers, and

dogs began combing the park for the mountain lion. After three days the hounds lost interest in the cold tracks, and the hunters abandoned their search.

When the *Los Angeles Times* asked Susan Mattern-Small to comment on this attack, she said, "I can't believe they would allow this to happen again."

●

Since I was a child, I have been fascinated by America's large predators—particularly wolves and mountain lions. The attacks on Laura Small and Justin Mellon received considerable publicity throughout Southern California. In newspapers and on television, wildlife experts from around the nation delivered opinions. I read and watched their commentary with fascination and horror.

But five years later my feelings about the incidents took a new turn. By then the Smalls' lawsuit against Orange County had wound through the California judicial system. Both parties had refused to settle out of court. Lawyers for the county insisted that a government could not be held responsible for the acts of a wild animal. The jury disagreed. They awarded Laura Small over $2 million in damages. Susan Mattern-Small received $75,000 for the pain and suffering she had endured from witnessing the attack on her daughter.

Orange County responded by banning all visitors under eighteen years of age from Caspers Wilderness Park.

These decisions started me thinking.

What if parks throughout our nation banned children because the wild lands within posed threats, however remote, to the safety of minors? How would that affect society's attitudes toward nature? Would my own love of wilderness ever have blossomed if, as a child, I had been banned from America's parks? To me it seems incontrovertible that when you walk into the woods, you accept risks, just as you accept the chance of death and dismemberment when you turn the ignition key in your car.

Perhaps even more unsettling, however, is what the jury's decision may reflect about our society. What does it mean when the courts—our institutional dispensers of wisdom—deem a government agency responsible for the behavior of one of the world's most mysterious wild creatures, an animal often described as "the perfect predator"?

At the time, I heard people blame this turn of events, like so many others, on "the lawyers." While an overabundance of attorneys surely has been a catalyst for the tidal wave of litigation strangling America, that sort of fingerpointing seems simplistic. After all, lawyers are just hired guns. They work for you and me.

No, the jury's decision suggests a far more fundamental problem—a society whose spiritual values are badly out of whack.

Of course, condemning "society" is as facile as blaming "the lawyers." To clarify my own beliefs, I decided to walk the trails of Orange County's man-hunting mountain lions. In Caspers Wilderness Park, I could put my money where my mouth is. Well, not exactly my money. What I'd be wagering with, to be precise, would be the large fleshy parts of my body. And maybe a few tasty internal organs.

As I walk, I think I will carry a large stick.

•

Biologists describe animals active during the twilight of dawn and dusk as *crepuscular.* Mountain lions are crepuscular, probably because they can hunt most effectively when deer are active—at dawn, dusk, and at night.

I, however, am not crepuscular. If I am awake at dawn, the

only thing I am hunting is coffee filters. But if I hope to glimpse the lions of Orange County, or even just experience their world, I figure I should be at Caspers Park at dawn. So one morning in January I drive south on the 405 freeway as the first glimmers of yellow silhouette the looming mass of Mount Santiago, commonly known as Saddleback, the most prominent peak in Orange County's Santa Ana Mountains.

The road from the freeway to Caspers Park is called the Ortega Highway. It is named after José Francisco Ortega, the chief scout for Gaspar de Portolá, who is believed to have traveled up the valley of San Juan Creek through what is today Caspers Wilderness Park.

The Ortega Highway cuts through the outskirts of flourishing San Juan Capistrano, passing numerous planned developments with names like Mission Hills, Mission Woods, Mission Glen, or The Hunt Club. Most of these bedroom enclaves are protected by a six-foot perimeter wall. Some have security guards posted at their gates. Clearly, the people who live around here are concerned about their safety. I wonder how many of them realize that a few miles away the hills shelter wild animals that can crunch a child's skull like it was a gumball.

At the risk of agitating the residents of Mission Hills, Mission Woods, and Mission Glen, I must report that their preserves are eminently accessible to a mountain lion. The big cats have been known to leap fifteen feet into the air from a standstill. (Take that, Michael Jordan.) They can jump more than forty-five feet horizontally. Keeping a mountain lion out of your neighborhood requires the walls of Folsom Prison.

Although mountain lions generally reside in remote wilderness areas, they do stray into human domains. In the last decade contacts between our two species have occurred with increasing frequency, often on our turf rather than the lion's.

The current scientific conception of mountain lions postulates that they normally steer clear of humans, and even other mountain lions. They are widely believed to be shy, elusive creatures. And most are. Mountain lions lead solitary lives, except for an occasional two- or three-week period when males and females live together to mate. The females mother their kittens for eighteen to twenty-four months. Other than that, mountain lions are the Greta Garbos of the high country.

A lion maintains what is called a home range, an expanse of land where it hunts, finds water, and rests. Depending on the abundance of game, a home range can vary in size from twenty square miles to over five hundred. The range must support an adequate amount of prey to sustain the lion, without that prey being annihilated by the lion's hunting. In other words, in an area like the Santa Anas, a mountain lion should be able to kill a deer every one to two weeks without exterminating the deer population.

While the territories of male and female mountain lions sometimes overlap (an arrangement that presumably helps the cats find each other when it is time to mate), the home ranges of males do not. When young mountain lions mature at around twenty months, they leave their mother's home range in search of their own.

So, many of the lions that wander into areas overrun with humans are young and searching for their own home range. But not all are young emigrants. Some are older lions, presumably with established home ranges. What drives these mature lions to prowl parking lots, golf courses, and suburban lanes is unclear.

Indeed, much of what motivates mountain lions remains murky. Far less is known about them than about other large predators like bears, wolves, and eagles. Because of their secretive behavior, mountain lions have mostly avoided scientific attention. Only in the past two decades have several major studies begun to reveal the predilections of the perfect predator.

Experts cannot even agree on what to call the animal. The "cat of many names," as it is sometimes called, has the widest range of any large mammal in the world; it has been known to thrive from the Canadian subarctic to Tierra del Fuego. The Indians of North and South America alone identify it with over forty names.

The most common English names are mountain lion, cougar, and puma. Cougar is a corruption of the Guaraní *cuguacuarana*. Puma comes from Quechua, a language of the Andes. Early American settlers tended to call the big cat a tyger. In Florida it is called a panther. Some Southerners still call it a painter, a variation of panther. In New England the mountain lion is often referred to as the catamount, or cat of the mountains. In Mexico and elsewhere in Latin America it is often called *león* or *leopardo*.

The mountain lion's Latin name, *Felis concolor* (cat of one color), was given to the animal by Carolus Linneaus, the father of taxonomy. This name is not disputed, although the classification of its twenty-six subspecies is. The mountain lion that inhabits most of California is *Felis concolor californica,* the Florida panther *Felis concolor coryi*. My favorite subspecies, from the lower Colorado River Valley, is *Felis concolor browni,* also known as the Yuma puma.

In Southern California small populations of mountain lions survive in several locations. Scientists believe ten to twelve mountain lions live in the Santa Monica Mountains, where they are partially protected by a patchwork of federal, state, and private park lands. In the last few years many people have spotted pumas outside the boundaries of these scattered preserves. In April 1992 an alert was issued for the Laurel Canyon area of Los Angeles—a neighborhood best known for rock stars and movie producers—when on two separate days a mountain lion was seen watching children at an elementary school. An Ojai couple found a dying mountain lion that had taken up residence in an abandoned doghouse in their backyard. In Granada Hills four mountain lions were spotted wandering the street. A Malibu resident stumbled upon two mountain lions mating in his backyard. When he shined a flashlight at them, they just stared back. He let them get on with their business.

In the Santa Ana Mountains, where they are mostly protected by the Cleveland National Forest, an estimated thirty-five lions survive. Like their cousins in the Santa Monica Mountains, these lions do not acknowledge any government-imposed boundaries. In Yorba Linda a lion was killed as she crouched near a hedge to watch children leaving school. A dozen mountain lions paid unwelcome visits to the posh community of San Clemente in 1992. Recently, a young male lion was killed on the Pomona Freeway, at least twelve miles from the nearest boundary of the national forest.

●

When I arrive at Caspers Wilderness Park, an employee is opening the front gate. This is Donna Krucki, a lanky, cheerful woman with sandy blond hair. I'm the first visitor of the day. As soon as I pull my car into the drive, I confront three huge signs in bold red print. In English and Spanish they scream out warnings of mountain lions, and they emphatically prohibit minors from entering the park.

I feel my resolve flicker. At the front gate, Donna passes me a small stack of documents. She says, "Read that and sign here."

"What is it?"

"A waiver of liability."

Moaning to myself about America's decline, I read the top page.

> You are entering a wilderness area characterized by certain *inherent dangers* [emphasis is theirs]. These dangers include mountain lions, rattlesnakes, poison oak and rugged terrain. Your safety cannot be guaranteed. Mountain lions are *unpredictable* and *dangerous*. Minors have been attacked without warning.

I consider the fact that I could be sitting at home right now drinking coffee and reading the funny papers. Posted outside the ranger's booth is a sign: Recent Mountain Lion Sighting.

"What's that mean?" I ask.

"Well, we think it might have just been a bobcat. The tracks looked kinda small. But when someone reports a sighting, we have to put up the sign and leave it there for a week or so."

As far as I know, no one has ever been eaten alive sitting at his dining table reading the newspaper. So why am I here, entering a wilderness park at some godforsaken crepuscular hour? I dash off my signature and waive all rights to sue Orange County for my wrongful death. If a mountain lion eats me, it will be fair and square. I will have done my duty as a link in the food chain.

Leaving the front gate, I drive past the children's play area. It's a beauty. Slides, jungle gym. All constructed of stout four-by-fours. Of course, for more than a year the play area has sat unused, bleaching under the California sun. As the waiver states, "Park use by adults (18 years) only. No minors allowed."

After my long drive to Orange County, I need to pee. I pass

the Visitors Center, but decide against using its bathroom. I remember reading in the *Los Angeles Times* that eight miles away, in Orange County's O'Neill Regional Park, another recreational area bordering the Santa Ana Mountains, a woman was sitting in a bathroom stall when a cougar poked its head under the door.

The woman, Linda King, climbed up the walls of the stall and hung from a ceiling pipe. "I was petrified," she told the *Times.* "I just stayed there and held my breath, didn't move, didn't blink. I acted like I was dead." After a few minutes, the cougar left. King was unharmed.

This morning I figure I'll urinate in the middle of some nice wide clearing.

Wildlife experts would say that Linda King, when interrupted at that awkward moment, did some things right and some things wrong.

One Canadian wildlife control officer, Douglas W. Pemble, when quoted in the *Times* advised that if you are attacked by a mountain lion, "the worst thing you can do is run. You must face the cat. You must keep eye contact. If they know you are retreating, it is to their advantage to go after you. With bears you can play dead. But if you do that with a cougar, you are going to be dead. . . . He is not attacking because he is mad. He is attacking because he wants to eat you."

Biologists provide lots of additional cautions, most of them directed at children. Zookeepers experienced with lions, tigers, leopards, and mountain lions speculate that these large cats do not perceive children as small humans. Instead, they seem to see children as a prey species—sort of like overgrown rabbits. Numerous zoo people suggest that when you take your kids to the zoo, follow the eyes of the lions and tigers. They're staring at your children.

Other experts offer additional explanations for the predatory behavior of mountain lions. Lee Fitzhugh, a scientist at the Fisheries and Wildlife Department of UC Davis, suggests that if you want to understand the killer instincts of a big cat, observe the behavior of a house cat. What most stimulates predatory behavior is a small object running straight away from the cat or at right angles to it. Fitzhugh thinks the running movement helps to trigger the cat's attack instinct. Children, of course, are always moving, often erratically. Just the type of motion that triggers an aggressive response in a cat. Worse, some scientists believe certain types of noises trigger attacks, such as the high-pitched chatter of children at play.

Cats, however, are usually apprehensive when creatures approach them from above. Wildlife experts advise you to look as *big* as possible if confronted by a mountain lion. Wave your arms over your head. Yell at them. Act predatory. If you run away, you're acting like prey, and they may treat you as such.

Mountain lions typically kill by springing on their victim from behind. They use their powerful forelegs to grab the head or neck of their prey, pulling it down and snapping the creature's neck. If the takedown does not kill their victim, mountain lions use their massive teeth and jaws to deliver a lethal bite to the head or neck.

Biologists suggest that bending or squatting in mountain lion country can be dangerous. You are, in effect, offering up your neck. Records of many attacks suggest that the victim was bending over.

Laura Small was looking for tadpoles.

Justin Mellon was tying his shoes.

A child in British Columbia was gathering berries.

A hunter near Vancouver faced off against a cougar, but when he stooped to grab a rock to throw at the lion, the animal attacked.

When I park my car at the trailhead, I slip out of my moccasins and into my hiking boots. Before opening the car door, I tie a sturdy double knot in the laces.

•

I step out of the car. Nearby rabbits hop across a grassy patch. The morning air is cold. I see my breath. For the last few days, warm dry winds have blown across Southern California. Despite that, I brought a heavy sweatshirt, and now I'm glad. It feels good in the chill air.

I start up the East Ridge Trail, which follows the summit of a gradually rising ridgeline. To the southeast the sun has only now cleared the highest peaks of the Santa Ana range, which forms a rugged back fence for the Marine base at Camp Pendleton. The world is still slightly gray. Everything feels cool and wet—downright crepuscular.

For two solid weeks before the desert winds started blowing, torrential rains—recording-breaking deluges—fell in Southern California. The hills have only just begun to dry out. On the East Ridge Trail, water trickles down a gully eroded into the dirt.

Thanks to the wet weather, the chaparral is again flourishing, after seven years of drought. Coastal sagebrush blankets the hills. Its threadlike leaves glow pale green. The pungent tang of wet sage suffuses the morning. Mmm mmm. Smells like roast chicken. Be still my salivary glands. The dense underbrush also includes prickly pear, toyon, Lord's candle, and lots of lemonadeberry, so named because its reddish, gummy fruits can be used to add a bitter flavor to drinks.

On the trail itself, which doubles as a firebreak, grass is growing, and in places moss is even creeping over the bare mud. Across the San Juan Valley, I see other firebreaks. The grass and moss on these distant trails glow chartreuse as they worm across the darker green of the chaparral.

The wet mud of the East Ridge Trail shows plenty of animal tracks, including innumerable deer. That's good, because where there's deer, there may be mountain lions. At least, I suppose that's good.

Normally, I would walk through countryside like this without giving it much thought. But knowing that the brush a few feet away could conceal an animal capable of snapping my neck with one blow sharpens my sensory capabilities, to say the least. In fact, it turns an ordinary hike into a minor test of courage.

I do not exaggerate when I say that a cougar could be concealed a few feet away. They are astonishingly elusive—when they want to be. Many hunters, scientists, and wildlife officers spend their lives in the wilds without ever seeing a mountain lion. Scientists tracking cougars outfitted with radio-transmitting collars have passed within fifteen feet of the big cats without finding them.

Behind me I hear *chick chick*. I whirl around.

I see nothing.

Paranoid, paranoid.

I'm carrying my walking stick again today, and I'm glad of it. Holding something that could double as a weapon makes me feel a little more secure.

Serious outdoor types will laugh at my timidity, of course. And they're right. In the wilds many people face true danger. I read about their exploits in magazines. I have even experienced some of those thrills myself—I've backpacked in high alpine regions; I've paddled canoes through some fairly dangerous white water. But today, the battle is not so much with Nature. It's with myself. After spending weeks reading about mountain lions and their unhappy relationship with humankind, I signed that release, assuring Orange County that I understood *mountain lions are unpredictable and dangerous.*

I have a flash of empathy with our ancestors. Humans do not like fear. (I'm not talking about teenagers packing onto roller coasters at Magic Mountain—that's adrenaline.) We do not relish the reasonable possibility that our life force will be snuffed out by the swat of some muscular paw. Hundreds of years ago, the first European settlers perceived the vast American wilderness as concealing many powerful, bloodstained paws. So for centuries they annihilated every predator they could find. Our forefathers hired men armed with high-powered rifles, trained packs of specially bred dogs, devised deadly steel traps, brewed lethal poisons—all to eliminate the vaguest possibility of mortal danger.

Today, the interesting question raised by that campaign is, Of what, exactly, were we so afraid? Certainly, the survival instinct didn't motivate this war of extermination. If that was the case, by now we surely would have launched hysterical campaigns to eliminate genuine threats to our well-being—like automobiles, electrical sockets, cigarettes, and handguns.

•

After walking for a half hour, I need to check the trail map. It's in my knapsack. Digging through the pack would be easier if I placed it on the ground. But then I'd be leaning down. Exposing my neck. Triggering the attack instinct. Here, kitty kitty.

Typically, after a kill, mountain lions first eat their victim's heart, lungs, and liver—presumably because those organs contain the most protein, fat, and vitamins.

I juggle my knapsack until I find the map.

The East Ridge Trail swings past a little bluff. I edge out to its lip and flush a big red-tailed hawk. It soars down from the hilltop, flaps its wings in a huff a few times, and circles away. Below me stretches the broad valley carved by San Juan Creek. Usually not much more than a brook, today the creek looks like a respectable western river—several channels braid across a broad, rocky floodplain. I can hear its waters rushing from here, half a mile away. Paralleling San Juan Creek is the Ortega Highway. Unfortunately, I can hear it too—the morning traffic grinds west from Temecula and the many other cookie-cutter communities that have encrusted the eastern foothills of the Santa Anas.

To the west, Santa Catalina Island rises through a yellow smudge of smog blown out to sea by the Santa Ana winds. To the south, ranges of crumpled hills stretch off into Camp Pendleton. In the early morning light their corrugations cast shadows across a hundred dark canyons.

I feel a distant vibration and see some big, twin-rotor Chinook helicopters clattering along the western horizon, heading for Camp Pendleton. They are followed in short order by some Cobra attack helicopters. A few minutes later a pair of FA-18s scream by. Standing in the chaparral, holding my stick, I stare up at these supersonic warriors. The ancient and the modern.

The Marines must be performing maneuvers, because all day I intermittently see and hear displays of military might. Occasionally, the hills shake from what sounds like heavy machine-gun fire, then the *boo-boom* of artillery.

•

I climb the East Ridge Trail for another half hour, and gradually the solitude and tranquility of the chaparral envelop me. I hear an assortment of birdcalls. The only one I can identify is the keening of hawks. A diverse assortment of birds flourishes here. (The Audubon Society maintains a large preserve, closed to the public, on land adjoining Caspers Park.) As I walk, I begin to relax about mountain lions. I spot some cat-like tracks in the muddy trail, but they seem too small for mountain lion. Maybe a bobcat.

I hear a sound in the bushes and whirl around. Nothing leaps out to snap my neck. Probably just a small animal.

Okay, so I'm not fully at ease.

Cougars are such skilled hunters, I probably would never hear one until it had sprung on me. A mountain lion's vision, hearing, and smell are so acute, it most likely would sense me a half mile away as I clumped into its neighborhood. If I were lucky enough to glimpse a mountain lion, the event would probably occur only at the behest of the cat, perhaps to satisfy its own curiosity.

Like domestic cats, cougars are reputed to be extremely inquisitive. Mountain lions often follow hikers for miles with no apparent harmful intent. Many reports tell of cougars poking their noses into unlikely places. Years ago a woman in Wyoming was stunned when a full-grown mountain lion jumped through the open window of her family's cabin. Suppressing the urge to scream, she sat motionless and prayed that her three children, sleeping beside her, would do the same. After exploring a little, the cougar lay down and nodded off, purring loudly. When the woman's husband came home and opened the door, the startled lion bowled him over as it abruptly departed. Evidently, the cougar was simply curious. It certainly wasn't hungry. Outside, the lion had earlier eaten the family's calf.

As I walk, if I am extremely lucky, I just might hear a cougar. They supposedly growl, mew, hiss, spit, chirp, peep, and whistle. But the cougar's most famous, and controversial, sound is its scream. The writer Robert Gray heard what he believed to be a caterwauling puma near his family's Rocky

Mountain ranch. "It sounded like a woman screaming in terror. A wild scream that rose higher and still higher, hanging . . . in the frozen air . . . echoing down the canyon and sending shivers up my back." Supreme Court Justice William O. Douglas, an avid outdoorsman, heard the scream of a cougar many times. He called it "a bloodcurdling screech—a cry that pierces the heart and creates a state of near panic."

The nature writer R. D. Lawrence *watched* a female cougar let out what he called a "great banshee scream." He says the sound must be heard to be appreciated. "To listen to such cries in the dead of night in wilderness country, where there is no other human being within thirty or forty miles, is an experience that causes the emotions to oscillate like the prongs of a tuning fork." Many scientists who have devoted their lives to the study of cougars have never heard this remarkable phenomenon. Despite abundant anecdotal evidence, some dismiss reports of the cougar's scream as tall tales.

The noises cats can make are linked to their taxonomic family. Most taxonomic experts believe that the cat family, as it evolved over history, split into two major branches. One, the *Panthera* genera, the so-called great cats, includes lions, tigers, leopards, and jaguars but not mountain lions. The other branch, *Felis*, includes most of the smaller felines—the house cat, the lynx, the bobcat, and the mountain lion, the largest member of the genus. The great cats can roar but cannot purr. The not-so-great cats cannot roar but can purr. The mountain lion can purr very loudly indeed. It may also be able to scream like a banshee.

●

I continue walking up a little grade.

A big noise explodes from the bushes beside me. I whirl around, raising my walking stick like a kendo sword.

It's a flock of quail.

About twenty of them rise from a prickly pear cactus and clatter away, sounding like an electric fan out of balance. The quail settle into the bushes fifty yards downhill.

I look at my baton poised in the air and laugh at my silliness. But I'm pleased too. I had the correct instinctive response. With stick raised high, I squared off against the quail. I made myself look *big*. I didn't run, showing those fowl the back of my neck, where they could easily deliver a death peck.

Down the hill the quail call to each other, "We-*scared*-him, we-*scared*-him."

●

Now the East Ridge steadily climbs, and the trail clings to its crest. Chaparral slopes down both sides of the ridge to valleys of oak and sycamore. To my left is Bell Creek, to the right San Juan.

At a high point on the trail, I resolve to be bold. I will sit down.

The sun is growing hot, so I peel off the sweatshirt, find a spot in the shade of a bush, and flop. Digging into my pack, I eat some trail mix and gulp water. A red-headed hummingbird darts by. I identify it as Anna's hummingbird, typically the only hummer seen in midwinter in the undeveloped portions of California.

With binoculars I sweep the valley around Bell Creek. I see no cougars. I do spot a pair of black-shouldered kites—medium-sized birds of prey—wheeling and diving at a huge hawk perched in a tree. The hawk, completely at its own leisure, dives from the branch, then flaps off toward the next mountain range.

I feel a sting on my leg and look down.

Red ants.

I jump up and dust them off my pants.

"See, it's not such a good idea to sit down," I say to no one in particular. I brush off my pack, shoulder it, and march on. Little itches swarm over my legs. I look down and see nothing. Now I'm not only paranoid about pumas, I'm also anxious about ants.

As I walk, I feel my shoelaces working loose.

Oh swell.

In the great mangrove forests at the mouth of the Ganges in India and Bangladesh, tigers kill humans every year. The victims of these man-eating tigers are often honey collectors, who travel through the forest, repeatedly stooping to pass under the low branches of the mangroves. Indian government authorities have provided masks to those who work the mangrove forests. The masks look like faces, and they are worn *on the back* of the head. Few of the two-faced honey collectors get eaten.

I forgot the mask for the back of my head. My shoelaces will just have to drag. No way will I bend down to tie them.

As the sunshine grows stronger, I climb to the summit of a small knob called Pointed Hill. Standing atop the little peak, I look down on the San Juan Valley and beyond to the ridges of the Santa Ana Mountains. Air, heated on the sun-baked hillside, rushes up the face of the slope and tousles my hair.

Feeling fairly relaxed again, I flop down and look around. I think, maybe I just need to spend more time outdoors. Months go by without my venturing into the wilds. If I renew my personal connection to Nature, I'm sure I will relax about its *inherent dangers.* Like I'm unwinding right now.

Of course, I'm on the top of a near-unassailable mountain peak.

From Pointed Hill the trail winds down into a small valley to the west. The East Ridge shelters me from the noises of the

Ortega Highway and Camp Pendleton. I hear only birdcalls and the tinkling of a small brook flowing through this little glen.

The vegetation grows taller. For the first time today I walk under trees. As the shadows in the surrounding brush darken, so does my imagination. Examining my park map does not help; it calls this path the Cougar Pass Trail.

The trail dips into a stand of oak trees lining the brook. Here in the deep shadows the air feels refreshingly cool and damp. Just this side of the stream, I come upon a big wash full of squishy brown mud. Big paw prints stride down the center of the wash. As soon as I see them, I say to myself, "Now those are dog tracks. I can see the claws."

I had read how to identify cougar tracks in Kevin Hansen's excellent survey of mountain lions—*Cougar: The American Lion.* The first step is to distinguish between feline and canine tracks. The tracks of dogs usually show nails.

As I look at the tracks, I remember the book said that sometimes cougars and bobcats will extend their retractable claws, but usually only when they are "walking upon slippery or disagreeable surfaces. The difference in what we see is significant—cat claw marks appear as sharply defined slits in contrast to the blunt impression of canid nails."

Well, this bowl of mud is as disagreeable a surface as any animal could slog through. And the claw marks are thin slits raked into the goop.

The prints are about three inches wide. If this is a dog, it's a *big* dog. But the size is about right for cougars, which have enormous feet. The stride between the footprints is approximately twenty to twenty-four inches. Again, long for a dog but consistent with a lion.

Hansen's book says that with a clean print, you can find definitive lion characteristics. The tracks in the muddy bowl look clean and sharp—like the animal passed this way within the last twenty-four hours. I start to squat to inspect them.

Then I think about the dense vegetation hovering over this narrow trail.

What lurks one bound away, camouflaged so well my ignorant human eyes could search the shadows all day without seeing a creature as large as myself?

Gooseberry-colored eyes. Studying my every move.

Pink nose drawing in my distinctive human scent.

I begin to feel that I'm not alone.

The hair rises on my neck.

Barry Lopez, in his wonderful work *Of Wolves and Men*, describes a phenomenon between the wolf and its prey—a moment when the hunter and the hunted lock eyes. He calls it the "conversation of death." Lopez thinks that "what transpires in those moments of staring is an exchange of information between predator and prey that either triggers a chase or defuses the hunt right there."

Inspired by Indian and Eskimo thinking, Lopez writes that the conversation of death "is a ceremonial exchange, the flesh of the hunted in exchange for respect for its spirit. In this way both animals, not the predator alone, choose for the encounter to end in death. There is . . . a sacred order in this."

Lopez compares these ideas to the way traditional Native Americans approached their own deaths. Those cultures, he says,

> stressed that there was nothing wrong with dying, one should only strive to die well, that is consciously choose to die even if it is inevitable. The greatest glory accrued to a warrior who acted with this kind of self-control in the very teeth of death. The ability to see death as less than tragic was rooted in a different perception of ego: a person was simultaneously in-

dispensable and dispensable (in an appropriate way) in the world. In the conversation of death is the striving for a death that is *appropriate*. I have lived a full life, says the prey. I am ready to die. . . . The death is mutually agreeable. The meat it produces has power, as though consecrated.

In the developed Western world, most of us lead secular lives, so we receive little guidance on the act of dying. Even those who do practice a faith will probably hear their priests, rabbis, and ministers talk plenty about the afterlife, but rarely will those same religious leaders address the messy process of getting there. Religions tell you how to live. It seems that one of their major functions should also be to teach you how to die. Secular skills—shopping or writing stern memos or manipulating strings of binary data—don't prepare us well for that eventual confrontation with eternity. When we have our own conversations of death—and usually our wolf is cancer or heart disease—most of us answer with a surprised and ignorant gaze.

Unfortunately, standing at this moment next to a set of fresh pawprints, I discover I am no better prepared for a life-and-death chitchat than most other Americans. Deciding not to expose my spinal cord to a pair of massive incisors, I instead pick a path along the edge of the muddy bowl and walk steadily and without panic up out of the cool, dim, oak-filled hollow. I do not further scrutinize the bushes. Frankly, I do not want to stare into a pair of gooseberry eyes.

A woman in Colorado recently engaged a mountain lion in a conversation of death. Like me, she was not ready to dish up her backside as consecrated meat. As described in the *Los Angeles Times* magazine, Lynda Walters, a medical student, was taking a study break by hiking a trail a few miles west of Boulder when she came face to face with a cougar. An outdoors enthusiast, Walters knew how to react. She backed away and yelled at the lion. The cougar advanced. She threw a rock and hit the lion. It didn't flinch. Then Walters saw another lion moving toward her and thought, "I'm gonna die."

She scrambled up the side of a hill, throwing rocks and branches at the lions, then scaled twelve feet up a ponderosa pine. One of the lions climbed up after Walters and swiped at her leg, cutting huge gashes in it. She kicked at the lion and, remarkably, knocked it from the tree. Using a branch she broke off, Walters stabbed at the second lion when it climbed up. She held the mountain lions at bay.

They paced beneath her perch for hours.

Finally, the big cats left and Walters was able to run to safety. She says, "I used to be pretty much of a bleeding-heart wildlife lover. I feel like at this point if I had to shoot a lion, I would."

●

Many Native Americans revered the mountain lion for its stealth and hunting prowess. For some tribes, the gall of a mountain lion had therapeutic value—it could instill the cat's ferocious nature into extremely ill people. The Indians of Southern California had a more practical reason for honoring the mountain lion—it helped to feed them. They would look for buzzards circling, which often marked the site of a lion's kill. If the carcass was fresh, the tribe would eat it.

Some Native Americans, however, like many modern men and women, found the mountain lion frightening and mysterious. One Dakota statement says that "whoever mutilates a mountain lion or a wildcat will have terrible things happen to him, like a dislocated foot or leg. Therefore nobody eats cats. They believe." Charles A. Eastman, a mixed-blood Dakota, elaborated on his people's attitudes. He said mountain lions "are unsociable, queer people. Their speech has no charm. They are very bashful and yet dangerous, for no animal can tell what they are up to. . . . He [the mountain lion] never makes any noise, for he has the right sort of moccasins."

For three centuries after Europeans first set foot in the Americas, they deemed the cougar to be "the lord of stealthy murder," as Theodore Roosevelt once wrote. This mysterious cat was the incarnation of the evil that lurked in the dim corners of the woods, just beyond the perimeters of civilization. In 1705 John Lawson, a Carolina surveyor, wrote that the big cats are "the greatest enemy to the planter of any vermine in Carolina." In 1738 the *Boston Gazette* expounded: "The Catamount has a Tail like a Lyon, its Legges are like a Bear's, its Claws like an Eagle, its Eyes like a Tyger and its Countenance a mixture of everything Fierce and Savage. He is exceedingly ravenous & devours all sorts of Creatures that come near."

These attitudes prevailed until about fifty years ago, when a new scientific construct emerged for understanding lions and other large predators. Often referred to as the sanitation theory, it held that the great predators are not really cruel killers—they are more like public servants. They prey on only the old and the sick. By killing weakened creatures, carnivores like mountain lions and wolves actually enhance the greater good of the preyed-upon species. They remove those individuals whose genetic stock and survival skills are not as robust as their peers.

Many biologists now believe that this theory, while partially true, is somewhat akin to a bleeding-heart liberal's view of predatory behavior. Unlike wolves, who pursue their prey and thus are more likely to weed out weakened members of a herd, mountain lions tend to hunt by stalking or ambush. Sometimes the animals they kill are indeed old and sick. But often the only afflictions that plague a creature killed by a cougar is that it passed too near on a night when the cat was hungry.

Mountain lions choose to prey on different species in different regions, suggesting that their choices may be determined by the lions' upbringing and experience. And they are learning new lessons today as human use of the land continues to evolve. A century ago mountains lions learned the hard way that man was the dominant predator. Seeking bounties, buckskin-clad hunters scoured the hills for cougars. But by the mid-1970s, state governments stopped paying bounties. Now the only humans scouring the hills are Gore-Tex–clad backpackers seeking solitude.

Some mountain lions choose to kill livestock. A cougar in Nevada once went on a rampage and killed 59 sheep and lambs. Another report tells of a single lion slaughtering 192 sheep in one night. While the severity of these incidents is extremely unusual, many ranchers and herders claim that lions menace their animals. Scientific surveys, however, show that ranchers' claims of devastating losses are exaggerated. In New Mexico and Nevada, where reliable studies have been performed, less than 1 percent of all livestock raisers report losses to predators. Of these, far fewer deaths are inflicted by cougars than by other predators, such as coyotes and even wild dogs. Furthermore, many of these predation losses can be attributed to questionable husbandry techniques. If you graze livestock unattended on National Forest land, whose fault is it when your sheep or cattle are killed by predators? Federal lands are chartered to provide pasturage *and* to protect wildlife.

In areas where mountain lions live close to human populations, some cats have also discovered the nutritive value of domestic pets. In Boulder County, Colorado, mountain lions and dogs have been engaged in at least thirty-seven contretemps. The county now has fifteen fewer dogs. Similar stories pepper the news from the edges of suburban LA. In the San Gabriel Valley, state wildlife officials recently shot a cougar believed to have killed three dogs. The officials stated that the cougar, because it had killed some pets, had seemingly lost its fear of humans. (The officials evidently had not lost their fear of cougars.)

Some mountain lions do seem to have lost their aversion to people—a trait that for centuries was assumed to be innate. Many lions no longer act secretive at all.

In 1986 a cougar in Big Pine, California, walked onto a woman's front porch and dragged away her English setter. When the woman fired two rifle shots into the air, the cougar responded by killing the woman's goat.

In 1992 a mountain lion stalked and cornered two hikers in the mountains above Altadena.

Also in 1992 an armed man in Placerville, California, sat on the roof of a barn to guard against a mountain lion that had been killing sheep. The lion in question, however, was curious—or just sociable. It jumped up on the roof of the barn to join the guard. As he fled, the man fired one shot. It missed.

In areas where they have not encountered humans acting like the dominant predator, mountain lions may indeed be emboldened. In fact, some cougars now seem to classify us not as a predator but as potential prey.

The earliest recorded killing of a white man by a mountain lion occurred in Chester County, Pennsylvania, in 1751. There a mountain lion ended the days of Phillip Tanner, age fifty-eight. Over the years of America's expansion, tales abounded of cougars attacking and killing humans. But evidence shows that the threat to humans has actually been small. Paul Beier, a wildlife ecologist at Northern Arizona University at Flagstaff, conducted a detailed review of all mountain lion attacks on humans in the United States and Canada between 1890 and 1990. He found eleven recorded fatalities and forty-six nonfatal attacks. Of these, almost two-thirds involved children. British Columbia holds the dubious distinction of attracting the most attacks on humans. Over half of all recorded mountain lion incidents have occurred there. In the last hundred years, four people have been killed and twenty-seven mauled in that province.

Since Beier made his study, three more fatal attacks have occurred in America. In 1991, an eighteen-year-old male jogger in Idaho Springs, Colorado, was slain. (Some authorities speculate he may have knelt to tie his shoes.) In 1994, a cougar killed a female jogger in the Sierra Nevada foothills. Later in the year a female hiker was killed by a mountain lion in the hills near San Diego. The two killings in California provided a good excuse for many television and newspaper reporters to churn up hysteria about the menace of mountain lions.

Almost since the moment Europeans first set foot on North America, their response to mountain lions and other large predators might best be described as a pogrom. As early as the 1500s, the Spanish priests in the Southwest offered Indians a bull for every cougar killed. American colonies began paying bounties on mountain lions in the 1600s. Hunting of pumas was widespread. An estimated six hundred cougars were slaughtered in a single county in Pennsylvania. The last puma in Pennsylvania was killed in 1891. By 1900 the mountain lion had been all but exterminated east of the Mississippi.

With the campaign against predators won in the East, America turned the war west. In 1915 the United States government entered the fray, sponsoring organized hunting, trapping, and poisoning campaigns. These efforts were led by

Animal Damage Control (ADC)—an agency sometimes termed "All Dead Critters." The feds killed over seven thousand cougars.

The private war was even more effective. On a hunting trip in 1901, Theodore Roosevelt killed fourteen mountain lions in five weeks. California's state hunter, Jay Bruce, killed seven hundred lions between 1914 and 1942. A Texas hunter named Ben Lilly killed thousands of mountain lions. He said he admired lions, but was "doing the Lord's work." Between 1907 and 1978, at least sixty-six thousand cougars were killed in the United States and Canada.

Even today, the cougar is not classified as an endangered species. (A subspecies, the Florida panther, is protected.) The mountain lion is legally hunted as a game animal in all western states but one and all the provinces of Canada. The exception is California. The California Wildlife Protection Act, passed by voters in 1990, bans all hunting of mountain lions except for individual animals that threaten humans or livestock. (After the two recent killings in California, some people, particularly hunting enthusiasts, quickly advocated repeal of the statute.) On the opposite end of the regulatory spectrum, Texas still classifies the mountain lion as a varmint. In the Lone Star State, anyone can kill a cougar any time.

Today in the Southwest, if you seek the thrill of bagging your own puma trophy, you can hire professional hunters for what is called a "will-call" hunt. Using trained dogs, often outfitted with radio telemetry equipment, these latter-day Daniel Boones can spare you the long dirty work of combing the hills for a mountain lion. Once the dogs find cougar spoor, they will track the cat. Thanks to the radio collars, the hunters have less risk of losing contact with their valuable hounds.

When trailed by dogs, the cougar, answering some ancient

instinct, will almost invariably climb a tree, despite the fact that if it turned and fought, it could make quick work of all but a large pack of hounds. The dogs will keep the cat treed, even if the deathwatch lasts days. Meanwhile, Daniel Boone will call you on his cellular phone. You can jet to the state, take a four-wheel drive to where the cat is trapped, and, answering to your own ancient instincts, make the kill.

Mountain lions have been wiped out across most of the continent but, in a few regions, they appear to have been rallying since state governments stopped paying bounties. Some biologists dispute the idea that mountain lion populations are rebounding. They point out that more people are entering wilderness areas, thus generating more human contact with the same number of cougars.

Persistent anecdotal accounts suggest mountain lions survive in parts of the Appalachians. In remote corners of the eastern forests, remnants of the original population may somehow have eluded the onslaught. Other cougars might possibly have wandered into New England from scattered populations that survive in eastern Canada. No physical evidence has been found to prove conclusively the existence of the eastern puma (excluding the Florida panther), although many skilled observers are certain they have spotted *Felis concolor.*

West of the Mississippi, the puma has largely vanished from the Great Plains, but it still seems to thrive in the Rocky Mountain and Pacific states. Based on surveys taken from animal tracks, biologists estimate that five thousand mountain lions inhabit California. They seem to flourish in areas of unbroken wilderness. Near urban areas, however, their populations are fragmented. As California's human numbers swell, more and more suburban lanes extend into terrain considered wilderness just a few years ago. This creates problems—for both pumas and pet poodles.

Mountain lions may have survived hunting, trapping, and poisoning, but they probably cannot tolerate living in the suburbs. As urban areas expand, mountain lion populations become separated from one another. Many of these isolated groups do not consist of enough individuals to survive. E. O. Wilson says that when a population drops below fifty, its viability is threatened by inbreeding, if defective genes are present, and also by simple acts of chance, such as disease, drought, or accident.

The total population of mountain lions in the Santa Ana Mountains is believed to be thirty to thirty-five. The cats there have established long thin home ranges that butt up against expanding residential subdivisions. Paul Beier says these lions will probably be extinct within twenty to thirty years unless wildlife corridors—stretches of undeveloped land through which wild animals can migrate—are maintained to connect the Santa Ana Mountains with some of Southern California's other dwindling wilderness areas.

Development threatens both of the corridors connecting to the Santa Ana Mountains. One corridor extends north to the Chino Hills. Beier's research has demonstrated that it functions as a wildlife link, but it connects the bulk of the Santa Ana range with only a relatively small undeveloped expanse. Furthermore, this link, which passes under the 91 freeway, is threatened by a planned subdivision and a proposal for yet another freeway.

The other more important wildlife corridor extends to the Santa Margarita River watershed to the southeast. It passes under Interstate 15, follows the route of Pechanga Creek, then skirts the edge of a subdivision and a golf course. This corridor, while not a proven means of mountain lion ingress, theoretically connects the Santa Anas to a large undeveloped region and dangles the prospect of survival for the Santa Anas' mountain lion population, especially if the natural state of this route can be restored in some spots and protected in others from further real estate development.

If the Chino Hills link is lost, the date of extermination for the mountain lions of the Santa Ana range probably moves a few years closer. If the link to the southeast is severed, the fate of these creatures is sealed.

Paul Beier bases his predictions on statistical models. Real circumstances, however, could easily prove his projections wrong and hasten the extinction of these cougars. Recently, the Santa Ana mountain lions seem to have been dealt more than their share of bad luck. Beier's study showed that they suffered a reproductive failure for three years, beginning in 1988, because of a shortage of males. Of the thirty-two cats Beier outfitted with radio collars, nine were struck by automobiles. Seven died. Donna Krucki, who participated in Beier's five-year study of the Santa Ana lions, said that in the month before my hike, four more lions had been killed on highways. Two of the dead lions were young males, presumably looking for new territories when they chose to cross the eight lanes of Interstate 15. Mountain lions are fully protected in California. That does not defend them from their main predator, the automobile.

Krucki told me, "One of those four was really a good cat. I'd been watching her for years. Some of these cats, they start killing livestock, showing up near people. You know they're gonna have trouble. But this one never caused any trouble. Never killed livestock. Most of the time she stayed up in Camp Pendleton. I'd watched her raise kittens. I got to know her like a friend."

Although we will not know for several years, luck may have already run out for the lions of the Santa Ana Mountains. The few cats that do survive there may simply be playing out an endgame.

•

Still following the Cougar Pass Trail, I climb out of the hollow that holds the muddy bowl of lion tracks. The sun now glares down on me. Turkey buzzards circle in hot updrafts. I'm happy to be wearing my big wide-brimmed hat. Anyone who has ever wondered why cowboys wear ten-gallon Stetsons has never spent a day under the southwestern sun.

I soon descend into a valley filled with classic California riparian vegetation. On both sides of Bell Creek, sycamores and oaks shelter a strip of land a few hundred yards wide. Under the trees the light scatters into patches of sun and shadow. Leaves rustle in a light wind. The air feels cool. Normally, I would exult in a sylvan retreat like this. Today, however, even after hours in the wild, I still find it hard to unwind. After all, *my safety cannot be guaranteed.*

I laugh at myself. All because I saw some signs of a mountain lion.

Well, they were more than signs. They were tracks. Fresh tracks.

What kind of woodsman am I?

Nervous.

I suppose it's easy for me to criticize the attitudes of our ancestors. I preach from the clean, safe pulpit of the late twentieth century. If I were an American pioneer, I too would probably be launching a pogrom against the "lord of stealthy murder."

Still, attitudes can change. Once upon a time our ancestors fed religious renegades to lions for a day's light entertainment.

•

Bell Creek tumbles down from a remote gorge high in the Santa Ana Mountains. The creek was named after a large boulder that once sat in the streambed. Indian petroglyphs covered the rock. When struck, the boulder rang like a bell and could be heard a mile away. To serve the greater good of Orange County, the eight-ton Bell Rock was moved to a museum in Santa Ana in 1936.

Hiking guides say the water in Bell Creek seldom tumbles down to its lower reaches. When my trail intersects one of these stretches, I find that the creek is not just running—it's roaring! It's raging! It's a veritable cataract. And judging from the reeds and bushes flattened to the ground for hundreds of feet around, a few days ago the creek ran dramatically higher.

On the far bank, the trail winds up into oak woodlands. In between is about thirty feet of fast, thigh-deep water surrounding a small island formed of rounded stones. Sycamores line the creek, their limbs bare, their bark bony white, mottled in places where the outermost layer has scaled away.

Looking for a better place to ford this "dry" creek bed, I crash downstream through the brush, all the while remaining especially alert. To my list of paranoid delusions, I now add poison oak and rattlesnakes. It must be that damn waiver. Normally, when I know I can sue someone, I enter the woods free of fear.

Downstream I find no potential spots for crossing Bell Creek. I reverse field and bushwhack upstream. Here I find a possibility. Only about ten feet of water separates me from the cobbled island in midstream. I wade out as far as I can without water slopping into my boots, plant my walking stick in the deeper water, and vault.

Success! I land on dry ground.

That stick comes in handy.

Of course, now I'm on an island. Immediately, I face the problem all islanders eventually confront. Options are limited.

I walk downstream looking for a crossing to the far bank. Nothing. I walk upstream. More nothingness. I head back downstream. Maybe I missed something.

Finally I pick the narrowest channel—about fifteen feet of open water. Throwing a rock the size of a saucepan into the shallows to use as a stepping-stone, I place one foot on it, plant my pole, and spring.

Failure! Both feet land in a foot of water.

I jitterbug ashore. Water gushes out of my boots.

It's time for lunch.

Sitting by the banks of the creek, I take off my boots and cotton socks, hoping they will miraculously dry over the course of a peanut butter sandwich. I gobble down this delicacy and chomp on some celery, which is still cool, crisp, watery, and wonderful. Finally, I crunch on a tart, refreshing apple. As I eat, I try to absorb the beauty of the spot. The sky is azure. Zephyrs brush my brow. The babbling water sparkles in the clear light.

Yet I keep swiveling, half expecting the gooseberry eyes. I'm sitting in an open spot, but mountain lions can leap forty feet in one bound.

I survive lunch and accept the futility of drying my footgear. Leather doesn't dry in a day, let alone a half hour. I lace the boots back up. (Double knots, of course.) Now waterlogged, they feel about five pounds heavier. Each.

The trail soon begins to resemble a boulder-choked riverbed. And that is exactly what it must have been a couple of weeks ago. When the water was high, the creek braided into several channels that wove across the valley floor—a vivid demonstration of what the term *floodplain* really means.

The trail climbs a few feet into denser woods. Here, the soil around the oak trees has washed away. Their gnarled roots look like thousands of writhing snakes. The roots are half camouflaged by dried leaves and grass that collected against them as debris-laden water coursed down the trail.

I arrive at another stream crossing. After scouting through the bush for a pontoon bridge or a ferry boat, I give up and accept that my losses will be small. Already I'm walking around in a pair of leather buckets. I roll up my pants and make a running start.

Not even close. Water up to my knees.

I trudge ashore. Water spurts out of the shoelace grommets.

Rolling my pants back down, I proceed. With wet shoes and socks binding to each other, my feet soon bristle with pain. I dream of peeling off these spongy instruments of torture and slipping on cozy, dry moccasins.

•

I trudge across open, parklike country dotted with mature trees. Big sycamores split into two or three trunks. Huge sprays of mistletoe hang from their branches. The limbs of fantastically contorted oaks arch over my path. They look like they're writhing in arboreal agony.

Along the trail little pebbles in the soil form the tops of tiny minarets. The rain has eroded two inches of dirt away from each little stone. There are thousands of pebbles. Together, they form a fantasy world in miniature.

Since 7:30 this Wednesday morning I haven't seen a soul, excluding Marine pilots. I am constantly amazed at how far from humanity you can get in Los Angeles if you just head out on a weekday. Then I see an orange pickup truck lurching down the trail toward me. At the wheel is a familiar face, Donna Krucki. She's inspecting trail erosion.

I tell her about the prints I saw along Cougar Pass Trail.

She responds, "They probably were lion tracks. I just saw some right down here by the creek." She points back to where I just crossed. "We've had a visitor. Male. Pretty good size."

She waves good-bye and drives on.

Her words ring in my mind.

They probably were lion tracks.

Right here in the middle of fifteen million human beings.

Gooseberry eyes.

●

I pass one magnificent old graybeard of an oak standing alone in a small clearing. Its knobby trunk measures at least twelve feet in circumference. The tree's great branches extend far out, then droop down almost to the ground. Together, these limbs form a majestic green dome.

Maybe here, under this fine-looking tree, is where I shall really test my beliefs. Here I'll throw down my money. In the shade of this great oak I will see if I can truly accept the way of the natural world and, for today at least, banish my anxieties. Here I will lie down with the lions.

The book of the prophet Isaiah describes a day when the wolf and the leopard and the lion shall lie down with the lambs. Today I think it is my task to act out a little part of this scriptural prophecy. I'm not sure which role I play as a human. Perhaps I'm the lamb. Anyway, today the lion will be played by himself.

At the base of the mighty oak, I check for ants. I see a couple of old anthills, but they look abandoned. The ants probably all drowned. The Old Testament talks about lying down with lions and lambs. It makes no mention of ants.

I sit, then stretch out. The ground is carpeted with dried oak leaves. Rather prickly, they aren't exactly a heavenly mattress. What is divine, however, is staring up at the tree. Its limbs stretch off in all directions and sway in a gentle breeze. The rustling leaves play a tune that dates from before time. Through gaps in my green arc of heaven, I see ravens rising on the afternoon air.

My thoughts drift to the terror of the little children. I imagine the horror they faced while hunting tadpoles or gathering berries. Laura Small has endured partial paralysis and numerous operations. She has trouble tying her shoes. Yet she told a reporter for the *Los Angeles Times* that for the most part, "I think I have pretty much put this behind me."

That's the strength of children. They're resilient. They adapt. They don't try to control their world because they know they can't. They don't struggle to understand that which is unexplainable, serendipitous, and at times even perversely malicious.

But we rational, educated, empowered adults demand an explanation. Insulated from the vagaries of fate, we no longer lean on God to understand. But understand we must. And since we have no better framework of beliefs, we blame it on the government. Or big business. Or lawyers.

Maybe one way to understand why the world can seem malicious, why innocents can indeed suffer, is to understand the natural world. There we can learn that death, even violent death, is not necessarily evil. Just as Native Americans developed an understanding of the cycle of life, we moderns must establish our own framework for understanding how, and why, death follows life.

Daily, we have less and less nature to learn from. Banning

children from parks means that young people with no other access to the natural world won't have a chance to learn from it until they are adults—when most of them will have finished forming their fundamental values.

We need to understand that in the wilds there live creatures like mountain lions. They are ignorant of our metaphysical beliefs, yet they are supremely knowledgeable about the ways of life and death. They are the walking embodiment of fate. They live by it, and they dispense it. As hard as humans have tried to impose their shifting value systems on mountain lions, the big cats have persevered—hunting, mating, raising young and, if they have enough land, even thriving. For me, knowing mountain lions are out in the wilds makes the world a little bit more like Eden, helps me understand why things are the way they are.

●

I awake. The afternoon shadows have lengthened. A chill creeps into the air. I lumber to my feet. After a nap on damp ground, the aging joints get stiff. In my clammy boots, I tramp on.

As I finish the last mile of my hike, I pass the area around Bell Creek where both Laura Small and Justin Mellon were attacked. As shadows from a nearby ridge creep over me, I sit on a rock. A few frogs croak.

I look upstream. For an instant I see a gray, ghostly shape. Its muscles ripple as it prances across the stream. The big cat stops to assess me. The eyes—those great green orbs—glow with a knowledge I cannot share. Then, with one bound the mountain lion disappears into the shadows.

No mountain lion crossed there, except in my mind's eye. Yet I know that for today, at least, the cat of many names is out there. And I know because of that, our world is a better place.

The Dark Constable

. . . . . .

When the first pulse of the earthquake hit at 4:31 in the morning, the building started chattering. Windows throbbed in their casings. Two-by-fours in the walls creaked as they rocked against nails that have held them upright for forty-five years. Pamela and I jerked awake, threw off the blankets, and leapt for the doorway.

Then the second pulse hit. The chattering cranked up into thundering booms, the sound of the building—and the city—bouncing on its foundation. Compounding the horrendous din was the noise of glass and ceramics shattering, furniture toppling, people screaming. Although my life didn't quite flash before my eyes, it seemed like it was cued up and ready to roll.

After the earth stopped moving, we pried our hands from the door frame and surveyed the situation. The building had stood. All that we had lost were material possessions—and a lot of plaster. At the time none of that seemed to matter. Material losses could be replaced. Vastly more important was the fact that we had survived, unharmed.

Soon afterward the words from a song came into my head—lines from a classic Mexican mariachi ballad, "Caminos de Guanajuato."

No vale nada la vida. La vida no vale nada. Nothing is worth life. Life is worth nothing.

We humans are flyspecks. All our edifices, possessions, plans, dreams—they are grains of sand cast to the wind when the Earth chooses to shrug its shoulders. Yet insignificant as we may be, nothing is worth relinquishing our flyspeck of a life spent here on Earth.

Within minutes KFWB News Radio was broadcasting earthquake information. Cal Tech, the seismic soothsayer of Southern California, calculated the epicenter to be located thirteen miles away, in the San Fernando Valley—an area called Northridge. Early reports gauged the strength of the temblor as 6.6 on the Richter scale.

When I heard these pronouncements I snarled, "You mean we lived through that and it wasn't even *the Big One?*"

•

The specter of an apocalyptic earthquake looms over the future of all Californians. Popularly known as "the Big One," this presumed catastrophe could hit a hundred years from now—or it could strike today. Seismologists say the Big One will result from the collision between two tectonic plates— pieces of the Earth's crust thousands of miles wide that move, often in opposing directions. Pressure builds up in the crust where plates collide. Occasionally the stress is relieved when the plates slip, releasing energy in the form of an earthquake.

The San Andreas fault, one of the biggest tectonic collision zones in the world, runs most of the length of California. Like myself, thirty million Californians have chosen to spend their brief days here on Earth within miles of the San Andreas fault—a force that could make those days substantially briefer.

I have always viewed earthquakes with healthy respect, but after January 17, 1994, they moved way up in my personal cosmology. Previously I had established my own system of classifying temblors. They came in two types: little and scary. The little ones prompted me to remark, "Hmm, it's an earthquake." The bigger ones sent me running for a doorway where I would pray to any divine entities that were tuned in, "Please stop please stop please stop."*

Up until January 17 the shaking had always stopped. But that morning, as the floor rolled beneath me like the deck of a sailboat, as I watched pictures leap from the walls—pictures I had installed to withstand an earthquake—I offered no commentary except an awestruck "my God."

One friend of mine, a dedicated Buddhist, told me after the earthquake, "I'm very proud of myself. My years of training paid off. When I realized what was happening, I calmly prepared myself for the death experience."

Regrettably I can't claim that kind of mental discipline. I evidently wasn't ready to relinquish the life experience.

•

In the days after January 17 I grew edgy and irritable. Though I hated being alone, when I was with other people I rarely laughed and often as not lapsed into silence. Incessantly my

* Some experts say a doorway isn't much of a safe haven in an earthquake. They point out that the door can slam on you. And running to the doorway—or anywhere for that matter—in a panic is dangerous. They suggest that if you're in bed, stay in bed. I don't know about the experts, but, personally, I'd like to die on my feet. I want to be ready to *move* just in case something big comes my way—like a wall unit, or the second story. Besides, I happen to know that bed isn't always so safe. On the morning of January 17 one friend of mine leapt for the door like me. When the shaking stopped, she discovered her low-slung, two-hundred-pound chest of drawers lying *on her bed.*

mind replayed those pre-dawn moments, especially the sound—the pounding that comes from everywhere. Sleep became nearly impossible. When I did doze off, I bolted awake at the slightest creak. During those long nights I frequently recalled a favorite line from Hemingway. As the war-scarred Jake Barnes observes in *The Sun Also Rises,* "It is awfully easy to be hard-boiled about everything in the daytime, but at night it is another thing."

Had I consulted a psychologist, I would mostly likely have been diagnosed as suffering from post-traumatic stress syndrome—normally the affliction of combat veterans and victims of violence. During the weeks after the quake, the appointment books of LA's mental health professionals were doubtless full, even without my business, because post-traumatic stress syndrome had instantly become a profound concern for hundreds of thousands of Angelenos. Well, it wasn't exactly instant. The pathology took thirty seconds to develop.

The passage of time helped a little, but hundreds of aftershocks only made matters worse. To hasten my psychological adjustment to a seismically active bedroom, I decided to confront my newfound fear of earthquakes. I would peer straight into the eyes of the Big One.

And that is what led me to be standing on the shore of a mountain lake, breathing the clean aroma of pine. A mile high in the San Gabriel Mountains, Jackson Lake is a small finger-shaped tarn that lies at the base of a long valley. As I watch the sun sparkle on the lake's rippling surface, I stand with one leg on the North American tectonic plate moving southeast, the other on the Pacific plate bound for the northwest. My legs are spreading apart at an average rate of one mile every 60,000 years.

When I was in college my geology professor assured me

and my classmates that no matter what your religious training may suggest, the ground does not open up during earthquakes and swallow people—be they sinners or saints. Standing here astride the fault, I certainly hope he was correct. He seemed knowledgeable, but I can't help questioning his guarantee when my flesh and bones would make a tasty tidbit to a tectonic plate awakening from a long nap.

The valley in which I stand is part of a region called the San Andreas rift zone, a series of valleys paralleling the southwestern boundary of the Mojave Desert and the northern edge of the Tehachapi, San Gabriel, and San Bernardino mountain ranges. For two centuries these mountains have blocked the northwestern advance of the city of Los Angeles. In the last twenty years, however, several hundred thousand pioneers willing to tolerate two-hour commutes broke through these topographic barriers. (They were led, of course, by those intrepid scouts, the real estate developers.) The region where many of these hyper-commuters settled, near the high-desert town of Palmdale, constitutes the seismic front lines—Tectonic Ground Zero. This was the region I hoped to explore. By spending some time there, I thought I might better understand the time bomb ticking beneath the California soil.

To reach the San Andreas rift zone from my house, I must traverse a freeway interchange where several bridges collapsed at 4:31 AM, January 17. In thirty seconds those two-hour commutes for thousands of high-desert dwellers turned into five-hour epic journeys. Each way.

Consequently, I plan to rise at 5:30 to get an early start on my hike. But when an aftershock shudders through the building at 4:45 AM, releasing about a cup of adrenaline into my bloodstream, I figure, Oh what the hell, I might as well leave now. Combat soldiers may be able to sleep minutes after a life-threatening experience, but I have not yet mastered that skill.

I beat the traffic easily, but when I arrive at the San Andreas rift zone and start scouting the landscape for an appropriate hike, I find none. Two continental land masses may be vying for supremacy here, but the casual observer could easily mistake the rift zone for just another far-flung suburb of LA, full of highways, roads, houses, exurbanites, and their dogs. Not to mention cattle, barbed wire, and Joshua trees.

Thwarted, I pull into the U.S. Forest Service Ranger Station in Valyermo to seek advice. Sheltered by big cottonwoods, Valyermo is a tiny hamlet situated on land that swells up from the flat floor of the Mojave Desert. Behind the town the land keeps rising and soon crumples into the rugged San Gabriel Mountains.

Inside the station I tell the rangers I want to hike the San Andreas fault. They cock their eyebrows at me.

"You're standing on it," says an older woman who works the front desk.

"I know. Does that bother you?" I ask.

"Don't matter none to me. If it goes, I'll just ride with it. I've been riding earthquakes since 1933."

After some discussion, a ranger and I finally agree that I should start hiking at Jackson Lake. From the map on the office wall, I note that the elevation at Jackson Lake is about 5,000 feet, so I ask him how much snow I will encounter on this morning in March.

"Oh, maybe a light dusting."

•

From Jackson Lake a path makes a short, steep ascent through big pines until it joins a jeep trail winding along the face of the

6,500-foot-high Piñon Ridge. A few miles to the northeast rises Table Mountain, its summit a couple of thousand feet lower. In the valley between the two mountains—where two continents are crashing into each other—it's so quiet I can hear a dog barking miles away.

Up on the jeep trail I find patchy snow. In places the "light dusting of snow" the ranger predicted is a foot deep. Elsewhere the ground is clear except for a carpet of brown oak leaves and rusty-colored ponderosa pine needles. Water has ponded in ruts along the trail, and at 10:00 this morning it's frozen hard. I tap my boot on the ice. It rattles like a loose window.

Black oak and ponderosa pine dominate the slopes of Piñon Ridge. The ponderosas grow large here; some must be a hundred feet tall. As the name of this mountain suggests, piñon pines also grow on these hillsides. Indians relished piñon pine nuts, and many of the tribes of the Great Basin founded their diets on them, just as California Indians depended on acorns. The original inhabitants of the San Gabriel Mountains must have been well fed indeed because fine dining abounds here. On these slopes they could gather both piñon pine nuts and the much-prized black oak acorn. Many Indians considered these to be the tastiest of all oak nuts. Since I have learned not to eat raw acorns, today I'll just have to trust the Indians' taste tests.

The limbs of the black oaks are bare at this time of year. These oaks are winter-deciduous, meaning they lose their leaves in the fall and winter. (In climates like Southern California, some trees are drought-deciduous; they lose their leaves during extended periods of extremely hot dry weather.) Looking up through the oak branches, I see deep blue sky.

Festooning the limbs of the black oak are large, healthy clumps of mistletoe. Hanging a sprig of mistletoe this big at your Christmas party could land your guests in jail on a morals charge. Mistletoe is a parasitic plant that sinks its roots beneath the bark of young branches. Typically it flourishes in the winter when the host tree is leafless and the sunshine unobstructed. Both the Indians of California and the Celts of pre-Christian Europe thought the spirit of the oak retreated into mistletoe during the winter. The holiday custom of hanging mistletoe in the home probably originated with our Celtic ancestors as they prepared for the rebirth of spring by bringing the spirit of the oak into their homes. Similar beliefs led some of our forebears to deck their halls with evergreens during winter.

As I keep walking, the dusting of snow grows deeper and more continuous. This will test my brand new Gore-Tex boots. After waiting seven years for my old hiking shoes to break in, I finally gave up and banished them to Boot Hell.

Generally, the snow here is crusty. If I walk carefully, most of the time I stay on the surface. Fortunately, some unknown hiker has preceded me. During the melting that occurs every day and the freezing every night, this hiker's footsteps have widened and frozen hard, leaving me a convenient trail across the deep snow. I follow these icy stepping-stones. When I veer from them, I crash through the thin frozen crust into the powdery snow below.

The terrain here has little underbrush, so the walking is easy except for the snow. Sometimes the oaks and ponderosa pines thin enough that I can see through the trees and out over the Mojave. The desert looks as flat as a parking lot for sixty miles. Five parallel roads run straight across it, but from my perspective they all seem to be aimed at a single vanishing point, lost in a distant haze. Floating above that haze, a few dim white peaks shimmer. The Sierras.

I shift my gaze down to the valley lying at my feet. It's innocuous. Pines cascade down my side of the San Andreas fault. On the other side of this valley, over yonder on the North American plate, juniper and yucca climb the slopes of Table Mountain.

I consider the havoc that will be unleashed when Table Mountain continues its jerky march north. A slip of ten or twenty feet could release as much energy as a five-megaton nuclear explosion. (The 1906 San Francisco earthquake triggered a slip of approximately twenty feet.) Seismologists say the shaking from a movement like that could last two minutes, maybe three. The duration of the shaking reflects the length of the fault that shifts. Many geologists suggest that a section of the San Andreas from San Bernardino to San Diego could jump all at once—a distance of close to a hundred miles. Faults tend to move in sections, and no stretch along that length has shifted in recorded history. Judging from geologic evidence, we're way overdue. If that whole section goes, some experts think the shaking could last seven minutes.

I hope I'm out of town.

Unfortunately I know all too well how long a mere thirty seconds can last. The first time you live through them, they go on *forever.* And then you relive them. And relive them. Several times a night. It doesn't matter if you experience a real earthquake or a dream earthquake. Your heart beats just as fast.

•

Under normal circumstances there's not much I enjoy more than watching a CNN reporter attempting to describe pictures of rain blowing horizontally past the camera while he peers out at the raging force of a hurricane. Or watching news footage of houses bobbing down some rain-swollen river. Call it perverse, but I have always loved a natural disaster. But

these days, in light of my newfound nervousness about earthquakes, my friends have been quick to ask if my love of disas-
ters extends to my own. The answer is . . . yes! While I am certainly chastened, I am not changed. I am just as fascinated by
the details of our catastrophe as anyone else's.

I love seeing geologists fumble to explain why one neighborhood in LA looks like Sarajevo while the next stands
unscathed.

I cackle with amusement when structural engineers grope
to explain why steel-frame buildings sustained so much structural damage—despite those engineers' earlier assurances
that these types of buildings were nearly "earthquake proof."

I feel a chill when I hear that people are vacating their
homes in the San Fernando Valley not because the ground
keeps moving, but because of the *sounds* it has been making.
For weeks residents there swore the Earth itself was creaking
and moaning. Some couldn't stand it and made arrangements
with U-Haul. Chalk one up for unbridled Nature.

Up on the mountaintops a distant wind whispers through
the pines. City boy that I am, when I first hear it, I think it's a
jet engine. But the murmuring gathers force as the wind gusts
down the slopes, then roars over me with a cold blast. Brown
pine needles rain down on me.

Yes, the world spins on, unhindered by human delusions.

The dusting of snow deepens, and the snow-covered jeep
road begins to blend with the snow-covered mountainsides.
It grows increasingly hard to follow. Sometimes I lose the road
entirely without even realizing it, and I walk beneath the trees
until a thicket of underbrush blocks my progress. Then I
must wander about looking for signs of the road. My predecessor on the trail, for whom I have developed enormous
affection, has long since turned back, leaving me to break

snow on my own. In summer, bushwhacking through open country under big oaks and pines like this would be a waltz. Today it's starting to resemble a death march.

I fall through the snow's surface and sink to my thighs. Snow crams down inside my boots. Gore-Tex can't do anything about that. What I need are snowshoes.

This wasn't the kind of San Andreas exploration I expected. I'd planned a desert hike. Come to think of it, I'm hauling nearly a gallon of water in my knapsack. When the ranger said "a dusting of snow," I figured that was manageable. Well, thanks to that dusting, my feet feel like someone spilled a pitcher of gin-and-tonic down my socks.

I try to focus on the joys of the experience. It's a spectacular, clear day. The air is infused with the smell of pine. The world smells like Christmas, and that makes me smile. The temperature is mild, except for the micro-climate developing inside my boots.

Birds fill the trees: chickadees, piñon jays, sapsuckers, acorn woodpeckers. I pass a huge ponderosa pine that the woodpeckers have adopted as an acorn granary. Holes perforate the tree's bark fifty or sixty feet into the air, far up into the tree's upper branches. Plenty of other birds flit through these trees too, but I don't recognize them.

As I walk through a shadowy stretch of the forest I hear, a long deep *hooo, hooo, hoooo.*

That could be a California spotted owl. Unlike most other members of their genus, spotted owls are sometimes diurnal. And the California spotted owl is more common than its controversial cousin, the northern spotted owl, the symbol for many people of everything that is bad about the environmental movement.

Personally, I'm thrilled. I feel a brush of mystery, like an unseen wing fluttering past my cheek on a dark night. I tingle with the same awe—and apprehension—humanity has felt for owls through the ages. In olden days the owl was sometimes dubbed "the constable from the dark land" because, according to many cultures around the world, it called for souls.

I hope this one isn't performing that role right now. If so, he's late. I expected him on January 17.

•

The hiking grows even more arduous. I trudge through a blanket of snow two feet deep. Most of the time I try to walk as though wearing snowshoes. Strike the crust of the snow as squarely as possible, exerting an even amount of weight across as broad an area as possible. That works, for a few steps. Then the ice cracks. I sink into deep powder and flail until I regain a firm footing.

What am I doing out here?

I just wanted to pay my respects to the Big One. I hoped to gain some understanding of this terrifying force, this stranger on the outskirts of town who walks softly but carries a five-megaton bomb. Unfortunately, try as I might, I can't ponder abstractions like the fate of my city when a stream of ice water is trickling through my toes.

Maybe the lesson I should be taking home today is that when it comes to Nature, I don't set the agenda. You ask for earthquakes, you get snow. The Earth has just told me, "I am not your therapist."

Nature isn't here to help us or to hinder us. Nature just is.

Thinking Nature can heal me probably shows as much folly on my part as the structural engineer who proclaims a building to be "earthquake safe." We humans may be extremely influential in controlling the shape of life on Earth, but ultimately we are merely tenants on this planet, not monarchs. Nature is not here to serve us. The system spins along with a momentum far beyond human control, or even human consciousness.

Believing that we hold enough might to rein in the Earth may well prove to be our species' fatal flaw. It's hubris. As all good literature majors know, hubris sank Oedipus, and in the end it will probably sink the human race too. Of course, ultimately Oedipus learned his lesson, and when the human race is wandering around in rags and blind (probably from overexposure to ultraviolet rays), perhaps we will have learned ours as well. Personally, I hope it's a little before then.

•

Walking back down Piñon Ridge is easier. My footprints have broken the snow. I just follow them. Insert the right foot into the old lefts. Insert the left foot into the old rights.

Standing again at the end of Jackson Lake, I watch a couple picnicking farther down the shore. Tethered nearby, their two dogs are barking like mad. Probably these pooches are agitated because they aren't eating, while the human couple gets first crack at the food. But what if they're yowling because of that oft-reported ability among animals to sense an imminent earthquake?

Except for that dissonant note, it's peaceful standing on the edge of the lake, listening to some ducks gabbling, smelling the pine, watching the sun flash on the rippling water, bridging two great tectonic plates with my oh-so-mortal legs.

When the time comes for the dark constable to call on me and I roll that private screening of my life story, I hope it's scenes like this that I'll be reviewing. These kind of moments convince a mere flyspeck like myself to clutch the door frame for as long as possible.

Dreaming the Land

· · · · · ·

Dozens of bridges span the city of Pittsburgh's three great rivers: the Allegheny, Monongahela, and Ohio. As a boy growing up there, I liked to play a game when I crossed any of those bridges. While staring out at the bleak industrial landscapes lining the rivers, I mentally stripped away the miles of hulking black steel mills belching flame and smoke. I erased the soot-stained brick buildings blanketing the floodplains, blotted out the clapboard houses clinging to the hills that slope down to the river. Even the bridge I was crossing would vanish.

In my mind all that remained was an unbroken wall of trees facing a channel of green water. Paddling a canoe up the wide, glassy river, I was the first person to lay eyes on this paradise.

I've continued this kind of game into adulthood. I still amuse myself by mentally undressing cities. But now I do most of my fantasizing in Los Angeles.

I like to picture the land in LA as it was decades—even centuries—ago. When I drive across Sepulveda Pass, I prefer to see the rugged canyon Gaspar de Portolá explored rather than a mountain valley sliced open by a ten-lane freeway. When I wind through Topanga Canyon, I ignore the offbeat suburban enclaves and instead traverse a boulder-strewn badland sheltering bandits and smugglers. I deconstruct neighborhoods like Santa Monica, Westwood, and Culver City— communities largely indistinguishable from one another, theoretical demarcations on the grid that is greater Los Angeles—and see them instead as small towns, splashes of light, connected by long dark stretches of country road. When I'm feeling especially mischievous, I turn the clock so far back that the skyscrapers of downtown LA are replaced by domed huts built of willow sticks—the Gabrieleño village of Yang-Na.

Unfortunately, in my more somber moments I fear that soon the only natural places surviving in Los Angeles—or anywhere in the world for that matter—will be those in my imagination. In ten years California's population will grow by five million, America's by fifty million, the earth's by *one billion*. We humans will poison so much land and water, grind up so much natural habitat, alter so profoundly the global systems upon which all life depends, I can't help but worry that humanity is headed for a reckoning. We have all been very naughty and if we don't change our ways, Mother Nature is going to take us on an apocalyptic trip to the woodshed.

Learning about the history of Los Angeles only reinforces my fears. For more than a century the fundamental business of Los Angeles has been the hawking of real estate. Buying a home is the dream of most Angelenos—as it is for most Americans—and innumerable developers have reaped fortunes by satisfying LA's seemingly endless demand for housing. Unfortunately, selling dreams by the square foot inflicts lasting damage on the natural world. Today, after a hundred years of rampant real estate speculation, two-bedroom starter homes blanket the land. Any shreds of Nature that cling to life amidst LA's sea of residential options usually have survived because some rich landowner resisted the entreaties of the real estate market for a decade or two longer than his or her neighbors.

Despite this sorry legacy, a few people in Los Angeles are playing the same kind of mental game in which I indulge. They too see the land the way it used to be. But remarkably, some of them aren't just daydreaming. They're actually *doing something about it.* These people think they can reverse our species' stampede to plaster the earth with concrete. They believe they can bring long-vanished landscapes back to life, starting right here in America's second-largest urban center. They proclaim that with great effort and expertise, they can make pieces of our city—not to mention the state, the country, and the continent—look much like it did when Gaspar de Portolá rode through on his mules in 1769.

One local prophet bold enough to preach this message of hope is Jon Earl, co-founder of a grassroots environmental organization named Rhapsody in Green. Earl, a lanky fellow with a boyish face, bubbles with enthusiasm when he talks about restoring wilderness. For several years Rhapsody in Green has focused on restoring a small preserve of open land known as the El Segundo sand dunes, but the group's real goal, Earl proclaims, "is nothing less than the 're-wilding' of Los Angeles."

That is a dream strikingly similar to the musings of a boy on a bridge in Pittsburgh.

•

On a cool gray day in May I arrive at the El Segundo dunes and stop my car outside a padlocked gate in a chain link fence. After a few minutes a battered brown Volvo stationwagon pulls up and Adriano Mattoni jumps out. A lean, wiry man dressed in jeans and work boots, Adriano unlocks two padlocks, shoves the gate open, slips his Volvo into neutral, pushes the car through, and waves me in. I ease my car into the preserve, and he chains the fence behind us.

Following the old Volvo up a hill into the dunes, I turn down a broad boulevard lined with sidewalks and concrete curbs. This could be any street in suburban America except for one small matter—all the houses are gone.

Foundation walls stand half buried in drifting sand. The tumbled remains of front porches provide sweeping views of the Pacific Ocean, but no one is here to enjoy the vista. A flight of stairs marches up a little knoll and presents a grand entrance to what was once someone's beloved home. Today the steps frame only tumbleweeds.

I feel as though I'm touring the ruins of a lost culture, but these decaying remains were not left behind by the Mayans or the Anasazi. They are remnants of my own culture—or, more accurately, my parents'.

What happened here? Where did everyone go?

Scholars of Old English literature have a term for the sensation I am experiencing: *Ubi sunt.* It's a Latin phrase meaning "where are they?" The texts that survive from the end of the first millennium in England are rife with references to a lordly but lost people. Ruins of magnificent Roman structures punctuated the English countryside. They stood abandoned because barbarians had stormed out of the European wilderness in the fourth and fifth centuries and sacked the Roman Empire. The Vandals and Visigoths smashed the culture and technology of Rome and plunged Europe into a thousand years of relative savagery. Centuries later, the people who lived among the crumbling Roman outposts on the British Isles could not dream of erecting structures half as grand. They referred to the lost Romans as "the giants."

No one would describe the people who lived here on the El Segundo dunes as giants. They did not erect heroic structures like Hadrian's Wall, nor did their centurions fend off attacks from fierce bands of Picts and Scots. The only barbarous forces these middle-class Americans battled were lawyers from the Los Angeles Department of Airports.

The residents of the El Segundo dunes had the misfortune of living next to a big and very powerful neighbor—Los Angeles International Airport, popularly known by its airline code, LAX. In the 1960s and '70s the U.S. government and the City of Los Angeles spent $60 million to condemn 822 family homes on the dunes. They bulldozed the structures, fenced off the land, and let the surviving plants and animals return to what they believed was a natural state.

Today the four main runways at LAX, the fourth-busiest airport in the world, launch a plane approximately every twenty-five seconds. DC-10s, MD-11s, A340s, 727s, 37s, 47s, 57s, 67s, and virtually every other type of commercial aircraft in use today scream low over the deserted sand hills.

•

As I follow Adriano's Volvo across the dunes, the only intact human structures I see are a couple of radar installations and a dilapidated trailer with dingy, corroded siding and a surfboard dangling from its roof. Adriano stops there, and I pull in behind him.

Sifting boxes, PVC piping, wheelbarrows, and five-gallon plastic buckets clutter the site. Drip irrigation piping snakes through thousands of seedlings stored in gardeners' flats flanking the trailer. Sheltering them, a gauze awning flaps in the wind. This is the headquarters of AgResearch, an organization led by Adriano's father, biologist Rudi Mattoni. Along with the rest of his AgResearch colleagues, Dr. Mattoni has proposed that the natural ecology of these dunes can be raised, like Lazarus, from the dead.

To render this modern-day miracle, AgResearch provides some of the labor and most of the scientific expertise. Bolstering their efforts are organizations like Rhapsody in Green. These groups have mustered more than a thousand volunteers, including myself, who descend on the dunes weekend mornings and contribute the bending, chopping, raking, weeding, planting, and watering necessary to breathe life back into an ecosystem that has run horrendously amuck.

•

If you have ever flown out of LAX (23 million passengers did in 1993), and you looked out the window, you probably saw the El Segundo sand dunes. As your plane lifted off, it crossed a sparsely traveled seven-lane highway, Pershing Drive, then passed over a few hundred yards of grassy meadow. The plane climbed to avoid the steep face of a sandy ridge that rises about fifty feet. As you gained altitude, you saw below a complex of city streets laid out in a rough grid across the ridge—the ghost of the suburb that once flourished here. Seconds later your plane crossed the western border of the dunes, Vista del Mar Boulevard, a four-lane thoroughfare, then flashed over the wide sands of Dockweiler State Beach. Soon you were high above Santa Monica Bay. If the day was clear, when your plane banked you could see the El Segundo dunes—essentially a single ridge of sand—extending about a mile from a large street called Imperial Highway on the south to a series of curving avenues that separate the dunes from a tract of suburban houses on the north.

This small reserve contains the biggest, and practically the only, surviving chunk of coastal sand dunes in the 425 miles between Point Conception, 40 miles northwest of Santa Barbara, and San Quintín, 100 miles south of Tijuana in Baja California. Seven major coastal dune systems once rimmed that stretch of shoreline. Today virtually every square foot of real estate along the tide line in Santa Barbara, Ventura, Los Angeles, Orange, and San Diego counties holds some sort of human structure.

At the 302-acre El Segundo dunes preserve, human activity destroyed 90 percent of the original ecosystem. Despite those past abuses and the dunes' proximity to LAX—one of the most prodigious hives of human activity anywhere in the world—this sandy ridge remains a hotspot of biological diversity. It is the principal haunt of the El Segundo blue butterfly, a federally listed endangered species. It is also home to the San Diego horned lizard, the ornate shrew, the western harvest mouse, the California vole, the sand dune tarantula, the south coast scarab beetle, the convex dunes scarab beetle, the globose dunes beetle, the dunes scaly parasitic plant, the Santa Monica dunes moth, River's dunes noctuid moth, Bob Ford's dunes pyralid, Lora Aborn's moth, Busck's gall moth, Henne's Eucosman moth, two varieties of *Scythris,* Belkin's dune tabanid fly, the El Segundo Jerusalem cricket, the El Segundo sand roach, Dorothy's El Segundo weevil, Lange's El Segundo weevil, the El Segundo goat moth, the El Segundo dunes cossid, and the El Segundo spineflower. All are candidates for federal listing as threatened or endangered species.

The list keeps growing. Irena Mendez, the project scientist for AgResearch, groans, "Everyone worries about the rain forest. But right next door to LAX we're finding species that haven't even been named."

•

At the AgResearch trailer Adriano Mattoni sits in a battered vinyl armchair missing one armrest and gives me a quick orientation. "Be careful where you walk. Try not to step on any horned lizards, or anything else for that matter." Adriano has a twangy voice, he's permanently sunburned, and his eyes are as blue as Paul Newman's. "Don't mess with the VOR [very high frequency omnidirectional range, a radar installation], and don't go too near the white canister on the hilltop near the VOR. It supposedly emits radiation. Definitely do not mess with the ILS [instrument landing system, another radar installation]. That's a federal offense. Touch that and you're screwing with a lot of people's lives . . ."

As he talks, I think how Adriano vaguely resembles a younger, skinny version of the character actor Richard Farnsworth. Their faces are shaped similarly and, like the actor, Adriano sports a luxurious mustache. The primary difference between the two is one of personal grooming—Mattoni wears a ponytail down to his shoulder blades.

Adriano Mattoni holds a job title once reserved for skilled technicians laboring over masterpieces of art or architecture. He is a restorationist. He spends his days at the El Segundo dunes attempting to resuscitate an ecosystem whose vital signs had flat-lined. Adriano gathers seeds from native plants, cultivates them in the nursery outside the AgResearch trailer, and then replants the seedlings throughout the dunes. He yanks out nonnative plants by the acre. Sometimes he takes a chain saw to them. Occasionally he even sprays herbicides. Mattoni traps animals that don't belong in the dunes and relocates them to less fragile habitats. In other wild areas he captures animals that once inhabited the dunes but were extirpated there. He releases his captives at the preserve, hoping that they, like many humans, will take to life at the beach.

Adriano Mattoni's hands are thick with calluses and permanently etched with dirt. Oozing blisters cover his palms and fingers. He says, "I would like to spend the rest of my working life here at the dunes."

After chatting with Adriano, I feel well oriented, so I say goodbye and pull on my knapsack. Above, heavy white clouds billow down from a thick ceiling of overcast, suggesting a storm could be blowing in from the Pacific, even though that would be most unusual for May in Los Angeles. Today I intend to hike a circular route around the perimeter of this small preserve. On the first leg of my journey I walk south from the trailer and follow a forty-foot-wide suburban-lane-turned-hiking-trail that ancient maps from the 1970s call Trask Avenue.

On both sides of Trask Avenue grasses wave in a light breeze. These are European imports, mostly a species called *Bromus diandrus,* also known as brome or ripgut. Anyone who has ever walked through grasslands in the western United States has probably gained some familiarity with this species. When you returned home, you extracted sharp pointed seeds—or foxtails—from your socks. Ranchers tend to call *B. diandrus* ripgut because the name describes how its seeds, when dry, affect the digestion of their grazing livestock.

Striking out across the ripgut, I attempt to modify the heel-heavy, white-man's gait I've been using to propel my feet for the last few decades. Instead I try to visualize myself as a wilderness scout—Natty Bumppo in Reeboks. With twenty-five threatened or endangered species roaming about, I must place each foot carefully. One careless step and, whoops, there goes the El Segundo goat moth! An ecosystem careens out of balance.

I climb to the top of a little hillock overlooking the steep eastern slope of the dunes. Before me stretches the vast array of LAX, four miles long, a mile and a half wide, a sea of concrete, steel, and human energy. On the runways huge airliners taxi back and forth. Trucks scurry about loading and servicing the planes. Amidst this colossal transportation machine, mere people register as something less than ants. This is late-twentieth-century human enterprise at its most highly tuned.

But it wasn't always this way.

When Europeans first settled here two centuries ago, the dominant form of aircraft in the region was the butterfly. The nine hundred square miles immediately to the north, south, and east of modern-day LAX—an area that today houses several million human beings—constituted an ecosystem biologists call the Los Angeles coastal prairie. Grasses covered rolling plains, and countless vernal pools dotted the landscape. The first Spanish settlers here ran cattle, horses, and sheep on the grasslands—after dispensing with the Indians, of course.

During a prolonged drought in the 1880s, the big ranchers lost thousands of head of livestock, so they turned their efforts to dry-land agriculture, raising mostly barley, corn, and beans. As recently as seventy-five years ago much of the land east of the El Segundo dunes was farmed. Then in 1927 a few men with money and a vision for the city's future decided to steer the course of development in this area away from corn and beans and toward aviation and interstate commerce.

At that time barnstorming pilots were landing their wood-and-canvas aircraft on a dirt runway in the bean fields several miles east of where I stand. This crude airstrip was called

Mines Field. The fate of the land near the El Segundo dunes veered in a new direction one day in September 1927, when a Ford trimotor aircraft landed at Mines Field. The plane was piloted by Charles Lindbergh.

Four months earlier Lindbergh had made the first solo nonstop flight across the Atlantic. Overnight he became the most celebrated man of the century. When Lindbergh first landed in Los Angeles, 200,000 fans greeted him. The crowd a few days later at Mines Field was smaller—just the Los Angeles press corps and some select citizens. A group of developers, including Harry Culver (namesake of Culver City), staged Lindbergh's flight that day to inaugurate scheduled airline service between Los Angeles and San Diego. To spice up the event, Will Rogers, the cowboy philosopher and humorist, co-piloted Lindbergh's plane. Thanks to this publicity stunt, the next day every businessman and politician in the city knew that Harry Culver and his friends planned to build themselves an airport.

The City of Los Angeles had already been studying sites for a municipal airport. One possibility was Mines Field. After Lucky Lindy touched down there, the strip in the bean fields overshadowed its many competitors. Within months the city made its decision: Mines Field was declared the best of twenty possible locales. Culver and the other moneymen who staged the Lindbergh event owned much of the land around Mines Field, and that land suddenly became much more valuable.

Despite the rapid growth near LAX, the El Segundo dunes, several miles away, escaped significant development until the middle of this century. Real estate did extend a few tentacles into the sand hills in 1928, when a subdivision was planned for the site and roads were built through the dunes. But only a handful of houses were completed before the stock market crashed in 1929, paralyzing speculative construction for the next ten years. World War II kept the lid on building for almost ten more. The dunes sat moribund—from the viewpoint of the real estate developer, if not the goat moth.

The goat moths were not so lucky in the years after World War II. The war had brought enormous prosperity to Los Angeles, and the city was growing at a rate of a thousand people per day. Los Angeles needed a bigger airport terminal to service more flights and longer runways to accommodate jet aircraft. The city bought all the land between Mines Field and the El Segundo dunes.

During the postwar era LAX also became the center of the city's flourishing aircraft manufacturing industry. The well-paid aviation workers needed housing, and the nearby El Segundo dunes provided prime seaside living. Most of the lots offered ocean views. Cool sea breezes moderated the desert climate and blew the smog inland—an important consideration by the 1940s. Within fifteen years a flourishing bedroom community of two thousand had taken root on the dunes.

As the amount of air traffic from LAX increased throughout the 1950s and '60s, the thunder of jet aircraft taking off over the El Segundo dunes became maddeningly familiar to the residents below. Every year these homeowners stepped up their complaints about the noise to city officials and the Federal Aviation Authority (FAA). Meanwhile the FAA had a worry of its own: Was it safe to allow so many planes to fly a few hundred feet above a densely populated community? Eventually the city and federal government solved both problems. They condemned the neighborhood on the El Segundo dunes.

Not surprisingly, many residents of the dunes did not want to relinquish their ocean views, despite the howling jet engines. For years they waged a fierce legal and political battle to hang on to their homes. The homeowners lost. During the 1970s bulldozers cleared the El Segundo sand dunes, one street at a time.

Standing atop the sand hills today, holding my ears as the planes scream overhead, I look out over the tarmac of the Los Angeles coastal prairie and my mind turns the table on LAX. I imagine a heavenly bulldozer the size of a 747 peeling away all traces of the airport. I replace the concrete Sahara before me with a sea of rippling grass. Cattle and horses graze on the shimmering plains. The prairie glows with wildflowers in bloom. For good measure I throw in a few grizzly bears. I figure, What the hell—it's the symbol of California. These days the American grizzly may be banished to Alaska, but two centuries ago the golden bear ranged freely across most of the Golden State, including the prairie before me.

But alas, LAX is here to stay, and the California grizzlies are long gone, except those prowling my imagination. I take consolation from the fact that at least I can walk among the same wildflowers *Ursus horribilis* once trod. Here on the steep back slope of the El Segundo dunes, the hillside quivers with the electric yellow of flowering beach primrose. The landscape is an impressionist painting come to life. The blossoms of bush lupine form pastel blue spikes. Chains of purple sand verbena dot the sand, and the ground is frosted with tiny white popcorn flowers. Even the petals of a few orange California poppies flutter in the breeze, although most are still folded. Like a lot of humans I know, poppies do not embrace the day until the sun shines brightly.

Despite the ravages inflicted on the dunes over the last forty years, a few scattered spots look much like they did in 1927 when Lindbergh circled in from San Diego. The patch I stand on has escaped farming, sand mining, road widening, airport construction, and residential development. Of the

302 acres in this preserve, 20 survived unscathed like this; another 19 acres came through partially intact.

These 39 scattered acres—an area roughly the size of Dodger Stadium—are the largest existing expanse of coastal dune ecosystem for 200 miles in either direction along the California shoreline. But even these 39 acres have suffered. A scientific survey in the late 1930s counted 91 species of plants and animals in the El Segundo dunes. Another count in 1988 turned up only 59, with 20 of those species consisting of fewer than 100 specimens. The plants and wildlife that survived the last five decades now provide scientists with a model of how a Southern California dune ecosystem should function. Even more important, they hold out a genetic lifeline that could save the entire ecosystem on this preserve from drowning in a tidal wave of alien species.

The person most responsible for identifying the value of these 39 acres is Rudi Mattoni, an entomologist by training. His life became entwined with the dunes thanks to a tiny blue butterfly that the federal government declared to be an endangered species in 1976. At the time only a few hundred of *Euphilotes bernardino allyni,* also known as the El Segundo blue butterfly, survived on fragments of dunes scattered around El Segundo.

Rudi Mattoni is a big man with a thick chest and a full shock of sandy hair going gray. His face is leathery, like a rancher who has spent much of his life outside. Mattoni has a flair for the dramatic. When he oversees volunteers working at the dunes, he's fond of wearing a pith helmet or a coolie hat. At times he smokes a meerschaum pipe. Mattoni says that for the El Segundo blue butterfly, "Nature is very hard, Nature is very tragic."

The butterfly's tragic life revolves around the flower of a single species, the dune buckwheat, *Eriogonum parvifolium.*

The El Segundo blue spends most of its life as a pupa buried in sand beneath a buckwheat plant. For a few weeks—sometimes only a few days—it takes wing and flits erratically from buckwheat to buckwheat. In that short time the El Segundo blue eats, mates, lays eggs, and dies—all on the flower heads of the dune buckwheat. When the larvae hatched from those eggs are ready to pupate, they drop from the flower head and bury themselves in the sand around the buckwheat. There they wait for the next summer.

Unfortunately, throughout the El Segundo dunes, another species of buckwheat, *E. fasciculatum,* commonly known as California buckwheat, was crowding out *E. parvifolium.* In the 1980s the research of Rudi Mattoni and another lepidopterist, Richard A. Arnold, revealed the significance of this buckwheat brouhaha: the blue butterfly's population was plummeting.

Airport officials had planted California buckwheat on the El Segundo dunes to prevent erosion after they cut away a portion of the fertile back dunes to widen and reroute Pershing Drive. With the best of intentions, those officials selected California buckwheat because it is a native—but it is not endemic to the El Segundo sand dunes. For the El Segundo blue the consequences were catastrophic. While other species of butterflies and moths eat various types of buckwheat, the El Segundo blue subsists exclusively on dune buckwheat; in fact, California buckwheat is toxic to the El Segundo blue. Worse still, California buckwheat flowers about a month earlier than the dune variety. This early bloom allowed competing species of butterflies and moths to establish themselves before the El Segundo blue could, and that timing enabled parasitic species, such as predatory wasps that feed off the larvae of butterflies, to also establish themselves. As California buckwheat spread across the dunes, the threats to the

El Segundo blue proliferated weeks before the endangered, but late-rising, butterfly could take flight in July. With each passing summer the butterfly's numbers dwindled.

Another threat to the butterfly's survival was also brewing in the 1980s, and this assault had little to do with predatory wasps. The Los Angeles Airport Commission decided to build a twenty-seven-hole golf course and a resort hotel on the El Segundo dunes. The land had been lying vacant—of humans, that is—since the city finished the condemnation proceedings. The airport proposed protecting eighty acres of the site as a butterfly preserve and using the remaining acreage for a golf course. This plan generated a storm of controversy, much of it led by a grassroots organization called Friends of the Dunes. The group's leader, Sallie Davison, declared, "To bring the paying public into an area that had been condemned, where people were forced from their homes, was completely outrageous." The endangered El Segundo blue provided a convenient rallying point for the many parties opposed to the airport's plans, often for reasons that had little to do with lepidoptera.

In 1985 the matter was heard by the California Coastal Commission, the agency that oversees development near the state's coastline. After learning of the plight of the butterfly and the strong community opposition, the commission chose to forestall the golf course and instructed the airport to take measures to protect the blue butterfly, as well as to study the needs of other wildlife inhabiting the El Segundo dunes. The airport hired Rudi Mattoni and AgResearch to take emergency measures to stabilize the butterfly's population. They also contracted with Mattoni to perform an exacting biological study of the dunes.

Mattoni's findings were bad news for LA golfers: The dunes shelter twenty-five rare species; they constitute the only major sand dune ecosystem in Southern California; and that ecological system is rapidly deteriorating due to an explosion of nonnative plants and animals. As Mattoni says, "They hired me to do a study because they wanted to build a golf course. Unfortunately, the data did not support that."

In 1991 the Los Angeles City Council, acting largely on the basis of Mattoni's study, voted that two hundred acres of the dunes must be permanently preserved, a decision over which some airport officials are still smarting. Mattoni received a grant of $400,000 from the city and the state and set about the massive job of restoring the natural balance of the El Segundo dunes.

•

About a year ago I spotted a note in the newspaper announcing that an organization with the delightful name of Rhapsody in Green needed volunteers to help restore the ecology of the El Segundo sand dunes. Here, I thought, was a chance to actually do something to help the environment, rather than merely whining about an impending apocalypse.

So one Sunday morning I fell in with sixty other volunteers—students, professionals, retirees—and raked dried ripgut under a blazing sun. After an hour I'd developed a monster blister on my thumb. After two hours I'd gained enormous respect for migrant farm laborers who swing a rake all day long under the brutal sun. After three hours I'd decided to volunteer again.

And I did, time after time. Today I stand on a hillside where in January I joined forty volunteers and pulled mustard. And pulled mustard. And pulled mustard. I remember this hill distinctly because after three hours of pulling that damn weed, my back was so tired I pushed on my knees to straighten myself and momentarily dislocated my kneecap. It hurt like hell. Five months later when I bump my leg the wrong way, the kneecap still pops out of place. It's yet another pernicious side effect of exotic species invading America.

At least I have not yet been stung by a scorpion. Adriano Mattoni cheerily tells me he's been stung thirteen times while clearing weeds. "I think I'm developing a tolerance." Explaining his bad luck, he says, "When you disturb the brush, the scorpions look for cover and tend to run up inside your pant leg." He adds, "They're not dangerous, unless you're allergic. They're not even as painful as a bee sting. It's mainly that scorpions look so nasty."

Just the same, I tuck the legs of my jeans inside my socks. Sure, it looks dorky, but there's no one here to pass judgment.

Soon I near the southern end of the preserve, the largest intact stretch of dunes on the site and another zone where the plantlife is rich and diverse. This area had the good fortune to be bought by the airport in 1950 for the purpose of installing the VOR. As a result it was never graded for housing and suffered only scattered affronts at the hands of the airport's engineers.

The VOR looks innocuous; it's a small building resembling a double-wide trailer. Crowning a nearby hill is the white canister that, according to Adriano, spews radiation— presumably the electromagnetic variety. The radar looks like a six-foot-tall automobile oil filter. I steer away from it. I don't need brain cancer this week.

The terrain here more closely matches my preconceptions of sand dunes. In many spots sand drifts like snow. In these areas—called blowouts—sand breaks loose of the vegetation stabilizing it and flows freely, driven east by the prevailing winds off the ocean. The sand blows until a plant, usually a burweed, *Ambrosia chamissonis,* takes root. Drifting sand gathers in the lee of its branches, forcing the bush to grow higher to stay clear of the latest accumulation. More plants, such as primrose and lupine, sprout around the burweed, and their roots further secure the hillside. Eventually a new hillock is formed.

One essential ingredient for the long-term health of a dune ecosystem is a constant supply of sand. Without it, the dune eventually blows away. Until a few decades ago the El Segundo dunes were replenished with sand from the beach, which in turn was nourished with sand carried from the mountains to the sea by the region's streams and rivers. But today those waterways are channelized and dammed, and the dunes are separated from the beach by the four lanes of Vista del Mar Boulevard. Rudi Mattoni estimates that the dunes will be starved of sand in about a hundred years, unless human intervention can provide a solution.

I tramp across small rolling hills of sand covered with ripples carved by the wind. No humans have passed this way, at least not since the last time a strong wind sculpted the face of this dune. Only a few tiny animal footprints disturb the sandy filigree.

I trudge up the loose sand of a blowout to a broad saddle in the dunes. From there I can see beyond the southern edge of the preserve to Hyperion—LA's state-of-the-art, way-behind-schedule waste treatment facility. Concrete igloo-shaped structures dot the site, interspersed with long, low-slung, concrete buildings resembling military bunkers. Hyperion looks like the surface of the *Star Wars* Death Star. A little farther down the coast rise the belching smokestacks of a power generation plant and some storage tanks for the big El Segundo oil refinery.

Once, this utterly industrial landscape was nothing but rolling hills of sand—just like the dunes where I stand. This part of the coastline started changing one day in 1911 when a few men with a vision took a trolley ride down the beach. The trolley was the Red Line, the transit system that once connected the many small cities of greater Los Angeles. Linking the towns of Venice and Redondo Beach, the Red Line extended south along the face of the El Segundo dunes. The men on the trolley that day were engineers for the Standard Oil Company. When they asked their streetcar driver to let them off in the middle of the dunes, he protested, "But there's nothing here."

"There will be," predicted one of the engineers.

They had chosen this site to build a major oil refinery. Standard Oil had already constructed a refinery at Point Richmond on the San Francisco Bay. The refinery these engineers eventually erected on the dunes lining Santa Monica Bay was named El Segundo (Spanish for "the second") because it was Standard Oil's second plant on the West Coast.

Today a few men and women with their own vision for the city's future suggest that the industrial wasteland I see before me holds the promise of environmental rebirth. Jon Earl of Rhapsody in Green says, "I think you never fully erase the original habitat that Nature spent millions of years creating." In this case he may be right. Both the waste treatment plant and the refinery hold fragments of dunes. Chevron—the corporate reincarnation of Standard Oil—ran a successful advertising campaign in the mid-1980s touting their efforts to protect a few El Segundo blue butterflies clinging to life on 1.6 acres of dunes within the refinery's grounds. That commercial inspired Ellen Petty, the other founder of Rhapsody in Green, to investigate working on the neighboring El Segundo dunes. Her partner, Jon Earl, reluctantly agreed to the idea, thinking "we would find some shrubs out there and maybe this butterfly if we were lucky." When Rhapsody did start working on the dunes, Earl conceded he was wrong. "We were convinced in a hurry that this place was incredible."

Jon Earl and Ellen Petty hope someday to establish a wildlife corridor connecting the El Segundo preserve to the dune fragments at the refinery and the waste treatment plant. Then they want to extend that corridor south for seven more miles to some other pockets of open country surviving on Palos Verdes peninsula. In the process they would forge a path through some of the most expensive real estate in Los Angeles.

More important, Earl and Petty want to establish a second corridor heading north from the El Segundo dunes. This passageway would link the dunes to another large undeveloped property, the Ballona wetlands, a fragment of Howard Hughes's old land holdings. The estuary for the Los Angeles River until a flood changed its course in 1890, the Ballona wetlands is the largest undeveloped parcel of land in the Los Angeles Basin and the only significant tidal marsh for thirty miles in either direction along the coast.

Wildlife corridors excite Jon Earl. When he talks about them, his words barely keep pace with his ideas. "There's already a strip of plants along the beach that's twenty-five to two hundred feet wide. It's mostly iceplant, but we've walked it, and there's native plants growing there too." A strip of vegetation twenty-five feet wide may not sound impressive, "but it's wide enough," Earl explains, "for the native butterflies to come zooming through." And if a few individuals do indeed zoom between dune fragments, that's enough to allow genetic mixing between populations of creatures that would otherwise be isolated on islands of wild country.

"Of course, we'll have to remove Vista del Mar Boulevard," Earl says. "It just has to go." He laughs. "I know these things sound crazy today," he adds, "but in the future we'll be much more sensitive to the environment and these ideas will make sense. The airport doesn't know it yet, but they're going to be landscaping with coastal prairie plants. [The neighboring city of] Manhattan Beach doesn't know it yet, but they are going to adopt the blue butterfly. Or maybe it will be Hermosa Beach, or El Segundo. Whichever town can claim it first. Areas will learn to herald their local nature and even profit by it."

Earl and Petty echo many of the ideas promoted by the Wildlands Project, an international organization of well-known conservation biologists and environmentalists (including Dave Foreman, one of the founders of Earth First!). Hoping to protect and restore huge tracts of wilderness throughout North America, the group wants to establish large buffer zones to shield these refuges and craft wildlife corridors that connect the many preserves. In the words of the leaders of the Wildlands Project:

> We live for the day when grizzlies in Chihuahua have an unbroken connection to grizzlies in Alaska; when gray wolf populations are continuous from New Mexico to Greenland; when vast unbroken forests and flowing plains again thrive and support pre-Columbian populations of plants and animals; when humans dwell with respect, harmony, and affection for the land, when we come to live no longer as strangers and aliens on this continent.

In Los Angeles the obstacles to achieving these kinds of goals are enormous, so a restorationist's short-term objectives must be smaller in scale—perhaps the size of a blue butterfly as compared to a grizzly bear. But in an era when visions of any size are few and far between, the efforts of Jon Earl and Ellen Petty strike me as bold indeed.

As I contemplate the future of the continent, I lower my eyes from the steel and concrete of the prospective grizzly habitat across the street and notice a big black insect on my arm. I quickly review. Does it look like a goat moth? No. A blue butterfly? No. Whatever it is, it's starting to suck my blood.

Whack. I swat at it, but miss.

Just as well. It could have been a Belkin's dune tabanid fly, a horsefly that's quite rare.

•

Walking toward the western perimeter of the preserve, I traverse a series of miniature valleys that run perpendicular to the beach. Some of these ravines hold rivers of flowing sand; others are choked with plant life. I pause in one vegetated hollow for a footgear cleanout. As I walk through the dunes, sand—lots of it—is somehow mysteriously sucked into my shoes, despite my continuing efforts to pad about like Natty Bumppo. Periodically so much sand builds up in my shoes, it starts to crowd out my feet. So I have to sit, take off my shoes *and my socks,* and dump cups of sand from each. I should have worn high-cut boots, but I figured this was easy terrain to hike. I didn't realize how much of that terrain would want to join me in my travels.

After excavating my toes, I recline against the hillside. The sand feels warm against my back. Down here in this little valley during one of the twenty-five-second gaps between jets taking off, I hear nothing but wind, waves, and the cawing of a crow. The dunes here explode with color: purple sand verbena, yellow primrose, orange dodder, white popcorn flower, and every shade of green under the sun—dark green, pale green, dusty green, olive green. For twenty-four seconds, this place seems pretty close to Eden.

Then a Varig DC-10 screams by overhead. The whine of its giant turbines vibrates the fillings in my teeth.

When I poke my head up from this sandy refuge, I look toward the ocean and face other reminders that my little oasis lies within the swarm of Los Angeles. Swimmers and surfers walk the beach. People taking lunch breaks park their cars along a low bluff overlooking the sand. Traffic races along Vista del Mar.

Jon Earl was right. That damn highway has to go. The dunes need the sand and the wildlife needs the unimpeded access. Mentally I airbrush Vista del Mar Boulevard out of existence. The cars racing up and down the highway vanish. Sand slopes down from the dunes to the waves, broken only by a few flowering morning glories.

Unfortunately, more than the road separates the dunes from the beach. A chain-link fence is also required to hold back the onslaught of humanity, and that fence is defended by the armed force of the airport police.

On several occasions recently the dunes have been vandalized. Mechanized barbarians driving all-terrain vehicles smashed through a gate at the northern end of the reserve—just across the street from half-million-dollar beach homes—and rampaged all over the preserve. They even circled the sensitive radar installations but did not harm them. The delicate little plants in the AgResearch nursery were not so lucky. The modern-day Visigoths steamrolled their big tires over hundreds of seedlings, crushing months of painstaking effort.

Adriano told me, "I'm an Earth First!er. I knew how to handle this. After the first night, I buried spikes in the sand by the gate. But I didn't know about ATV tires, so the next night the spikes evidently got them but didn't take them out." He shakes his head with disgust. "It really pisses me off. They were driving around up here with headlights on, and the airport police didn't even see them. What do they do, go into the airport at night and hang around the coffee shop? Those idiots were messing with the ILS. That's a federal offense. They should've brought in the FBI."

Strange that the forces of civilization now huddle in the earth's wild corners while the barbarians live in the suburbs.

•

Leaving the undeveloped area behind, I cross what used to be known as Killgore Street. Again I stroll down blocks haunted by the ghost of Beaver Cleaver. Taking a seat on the curb, I wonder who they were, this lost tribe of suburbanites.

Ubi sunt?

During the previous weeks I explored some archives maintained by the LAX public relations department. My research revealed that the lot where I now sit, 233 Killgore Street, once belonged to a couple named Eugene and Helen Church. In 1969 the Churches and 372 of their neighbors were notified that the Los Angeles Department of Airports planned to seize their homes. These unlucky property owners fought that decision—in court, in city hall, and in the press. But finally they could fight no longer. They were all forced to leave.

On the day Helen and Eugene Church gave up their home, they mailed a letter to the Department of Airports. "Here," they wrote, "is where we planned to live and die."

> We covered many miles up and down the coastline in 1949 before we chose this location and bought the lot (a few months after we were married); the countless nights, days and sleepless nights we spent, plotting, planning, drawing up plans for our "dream house" cannot be expressed in writing.
>
> This is the end of the most important phase in our lives. We were not blessed with children—our home was like that to us. We brought it up from a mere baby—now, back to dust

this once happy home will go to. It's like having lost a major part of ourselves. . . . because every part of us is here—here in the creation of "our home."

I can see why they loved it. From their front window the Churches must have watched the combers breaking on the beach, each wave slanting south across the bay toward the hills of Palos Verdes. Their house faced an unbroken hillside that glowed all spring with poppies, lupine, deerweed, and primrose. When the Churches stepped into their front yard they saw the Pacific Ocean stretching to the horizon. They lived with the sea in all of its many moods—a colossal theater of water and clouds.

Today, mountains of uprooted iceplant, yanked out as part of the AgResearch restoration efforts, are stacked on the Churches' lot. Decomposing into dust, the iceplant blends with concrete rubble—all that remains of Eugene and Helen Church's dream house.

The Churches ended their letter like this:

You will find attached hereto "our last possession" in connection with our home—our keys. Our keys for you to enter and do with *whatever you please* to our home. Destroy it, sell it. . . . God only knows what; and God only knows, its ultimate fate we'd rather not know about.

The ultimate fate of the Churches' home may not be as awful as they feared. Thanks to the California Coastal Commission, the Friends of the Dunes, the Los Angeles City Council, and a host of other players in the arena of environmental politics, no one else is gaining from their loss—except, of course, the airline passengers soaring overhead. Today dune buckwheat colonizes the Churches' side of Killgore Street. The El Segundo blue butterfly flits by every summer.

Horned lizards stoically observe the passing of life, when they're not busy gobbling ants.

In 1969 no one ever dreamed that by bulldozing homes like the Churches', the Department of Airports would be bettering the lot of an endangered species. Back then not even ardent environmentalists were fighting to save butterflies. The only endangered species most people had ever heard of was the bald eagle. Yet the El Segundo blue butterfly and twenty-five other rare species at the dunes have been the primary beneficiaries of the airport's condemnation proceedings.

Although this peculiar turn of events probably does little to lessen the pain of the Churches, it may be a harbinger of future trends. In years to come we may choose to secure other flight paths—not for 747s but for birds and bats and butterflies, and the ecosystems that sustain them. We may not even have to condemn the land. People may gladly turn their yards and farms and ranches into habitat suitable for wild creatures. Some may even willingly deed away their property for the higher purpose of wilderness preservation. While this may sound like wishful thinking, a few people around the country are doing just that. Every month citizens ensure that their property remains wild forever by donating it to organizations like the Nature Conservancy.

Michael Soulé, a noted conservation biologist and one of the founders of the Wildlands Project, suggests that environmentalists can encourage this trend. He recommends they abandon their confrontational techniques. Instead, environmentalists should educate property owners about the ecological importance of their land and involve those owners in land-use planning processes. Even more important, Soulé advises environmentalists to learn patience. By adopting a farsighted approach to conservation, they may convince many owners to protect their property by donating it to some type of land trust—not right away, but on a distant date in the future, such as after the deaths of their children. In most situations Nature can wait that long. So must anxious environmentalists. "The key," says Soulé, "is thinking BIG, both in space and time."

•

I walk north along the former Rindge Avenue and pass streets that curve down the face of the dunes toward Vista del Mar and the beach. One of them is Grand Pre, a boulevard that in 1965 formed the stately entrance to this community. Grand Pre's wide median strip was planted with rows of big *Washingtonia* and Canary Island date palms. No doubt some long-lost developer thought this grand concourse would add an exclusive aura to the neighborhood. It probably worked. I bet the residents here took great pride in motoring under the big palms to their homes overlooking the Pacific.

Now Grand Pre lies waist-deep in palm fronds, plant litter, and mounds of brick and concrete rubble. An alligator lizard scuttles across the pavement and takes shelter in debris heaped at the curb.

I wade across a mountain of dead iceplant, walk between half-tumbled masonry walls, and climb someone's steps to a front porch—all that remains of a fine seaside home. Now the most prominent feature on the lot is a vine called *calabazilla,* or stinking gourd, twining through the debris. Stinking gourd—so named because of its foul-smelling foliage—bears a fruit that is round, smooth, hard, and a little smaller than a softball. Spanish ladies used them as darning balls.

Ubi sunt?

Amid the rubble left on this block, I find a shard of an ancient 7-Up bottle in the sand. Painted on it is the company's old slogan, "Try it, you'll like it." One glance at the bottle unleashes a flood of memories. I think of car trips in my family's old Plymouth—the one with the fins. I remember stopping at dusty roadside Sinclair stations in the deep South and drinking ice-cold 7-Up.

Of course it makes sense that this artifact of a lost community reminds me of my childhood. Although my home was a place of far more modest means—I grew up with kids who had never seen the Atlantic, let alone the exotic Pacific—all of my neighbors would recognize this suburb overlooking Santa Monica Bay because this kind of community spawned many of the myths that defined my generation. This was the land of capri pants and flip hairdos, Frigidaires and Pepsodent, blond hair and deep tans, surfer songs and Gidget. In the 1960s the California Dream—fun, freedom, and the thinly veiled promise of sex—was the American Dream.

•

A green Russian thistle sprouts from the debris along Grand Pre. Doing the dune ecosystem and my fellow volunteers a favor, I yank it out while the tumbleweed is still young. You must intervene early in the annual cycle of the tumbleweed. If the bush dries out and starts rolling rolling rolling, the plant will have a chance to scatter its fifty thousand seeds. It takes a lot of volunteer labor to counteract the impact of a single tumbling tumbleweed.

Unfortunately, the blocks around here still need plenty of attention. Generally, where the native foliage has not been disturbed, the plant cover has the hardiness to resist intrusion by most alien species. But when you bulldoze a three-bedroom house, it's difficult not to disturb a site. Now whole city blocks that once held homes are blanketed with the green tumescent fingers of iceplant. Each stalk is rimmed with red, like the bleary slit of a drunkard's eye.

Before AgResearch, Rhapsody in Green, and several other organizations turned their attention to the El Segundo dunes, these hills were rapidly mutating into an eerie savanna composed almost exclusively of two exotic species: iceplant and acacia. Transplanted from its native South Africa and freed of the natural forces inhibiting its spread there, iceplant ran wild over the turned-up soil on the El Segundo dunes, extending its range by a cancerous 30 percent a year. And yet the threat it posed was small compared that of acacia, which can invade disturbed and undisturbed terrain with equal ease. The roots of the acacia fix nitrogen in the sandy earth, thus altering soil texture and chemistry and eventually reconstituting the basis of the native ecosystem. Plus, acacia seeds can survive for decades. So even when you cut down every last tree, new acacias keep stepping to the fore. They're like the mythological Sparti, soldiers sprung from the dragon's teeth that Jason and his Argonauts slew to secure the Golden Fleece.

The ecological argonaut Rudi Mattoni says, "Biologists in Australia have told me, when we really want to control the acacia they'll fix us up. They've isolated a virus that's specific to the acacia. It really hammers them."

If only a biologist had sailed with Jason.

For now the AgResearch forces fight their Sparti with chain saws. Adriano Mattoni has cut down almost every acacia on the dunes. The El Segundo dunes hide many incongruous stacks of neatly cut firewood. Mattoni has also cleared acres and acres of iceplant. On some stretches he has applied herbicides to the South African menace. (Alien species pose a far greater threat to the dunes than does a single application of herbicide.) For the most part, however, Adriano and the volunteers rip out vast stretches of iceplant by hand.

Uprooting iceplant can be a satisfying pastime. Grab hold of a tendril, pull firmly, and long shoots unzip from the sand.

Rhapsody in Green has unleashed battalions of volunteers who spend half a Sunday unzipping a single city block. By afternoon they leave the site denuded except for haystacks of iceplant tendrils. "We're de-evolutionists," Jon Earl declares.

Once a site is cleared of the most dangerous invasives, native plants are reintroduced. I inspect a block where I spent a Sunday with thirty other volunteers planting seedlings. That day I planted bush sunflower, *Encelia californica*, a shrub with showy golden blossoms. They look like a cross between a sunflower and a black-eyed Susan. Although this species is common along California roadsides, before the restoration of the dunes began, only eighteen individuals survived throughout the entire site. That Sunday I personally planted forty, and they all seem to be thriving.

•

In the northwest corner of the preserve I trudge across many blocks of land that need lots of love. Acres and acres lie disrupted and forlorn. Invasive alien species abound. Fields of wild mustard have withered and set their granular seeds. Next March a mist of pale golden mustard blossoms will again float over this hillside. Storksbill carpets large stretches, its seeds just beginning to dry into sinister corkscrews.

I pass the remains of what once was the most notable home in the dunes. During World War I, James Donahue, a medalist in the 1912 Olympics and later a Los Angeles real estate entrepreneur, met a Red Cross nurse named Claire. At the time her headquarters was a castle outside of Paris that belonged to the dancer Isadora Duncan. There James and Claire fell in love. When they later married, Donahue recreated Isadora Duncan's castle for his bride on the hills overlooking the Pacific.

For decades the Donahue home, known throughout the

community as "the Castle," was the scene of glittering parties. The Castle sat on a small rise just a short sprint from the breakers crashing onto the sand. In the 1930s, when little separated the beach from the dunes, more than one of the Donahues' famous parties must have ended with moonlight romps in the waves. Amid the roar of the jets, I can almost hear the squeals of laughter, the champagne glasses tinkling. But the only artifact I find today of the fifteen-room castle is a single white hexagonal bathroom tile.

Ubi sunt?

A few blocks farther on, I reach Sandpiper Street, the northern perimeter of the preserve. If Jon Earl's dreams come true some day, here is where migrating wildlife would ply a natural corridor to the Ballona wetlands a half mile to the north.

A few weeks earlier I walked a ragged strip of vegetation just east of the beach—the route Earl's corridor would most likely follow. It looked like a tough commute for migrating butterflies, let alone grizzly bears. If *Ursus horribilis* had the urge to traverse this corridor, it would probably sniff disdainfully at the cigarette butts and Styrofoam mixed into the sand. It might claw at the plants growing here—Russian thistle, iceplant, acacia, ripgut. Lots of vegetation flourishes along this strip, but not a single plant is native.

Heading north, the grizzly would soon find its right-of-way runs smack into the wall of a beachfront condominium, which is followed by twenty more houses packed in shoulder to shoulder. The bear would have to lumber out onto the beach, where there's not a shred of cover, or else crash through the back decks of the condos, swatting aside sand buckets and surf boards.

Once past the beach homes, however, the grizzly could

stroll across a little patch of dunes still sparkling with native primrose (here the great beast might loose a snort of relief), cross a small street, and finally lope through a parking lot, a basketball court, and a grassy field until it stood facing a channel of seawater that connects Marina Del Rey, the huge marina complex serving Los Angeles, with the Ballona wetlands. Following the channel east, the bear would have a clear shot at more than three miles of open land—probably not enough range to support a thousand-pound omnivore, but plenty for a butterfly smaller than your thumbnail.

I broaden my *ubi sunt*-ing to consider not just the people who once walked these dunes but also the wildlife. Where are the quail, the plover, and the least tern that nested along this coast? Where are the kit fox, the weasel, the badger, the mule deer? And where is the big guy, the grizzly bear?

Currently the only region in the lower forty-eight states where the grizzly survives is the northern Rocky Mountains. A few true believers claim a lost colony of grizzlies clings to life in the high country of southwestern Colorado. I certainly hope so. In any case, it will take one honking big wildlife corridor to usher the grizzly bear back to Southern California. I doubt that will happen in my lifetime, but that doesn't mean it never will.

To bulldoze twenty expensive beachfront homes just to make life easier for a goat moth (and by extension, the grizzly) would certainly call for a dramatic shift in our cultural values. But Jon Earl is thinking BIG. For now, the creatures living at the dunes and the wetlands probably can survive without the corridor. But they can't hang on forever, and Earl is planning for that eventuality. He is laying the theoretical groundwork. He is planting the necessary ideas, if not the seeds themselves.

•

I make my way along the fence at the northern end of the preserve, picking through beer cans and even a few champagne corks. Evidently, people have a good time here along Sandpiper Street. But times have changed since the days of the Donahues' elegant parties. These champagne corks are plastic.

Soon I reach the gate where the ATV-mounted vandals crashed through. Adriano says he's ready for them the next time. I look for signs of spikes hidden in the sand. All I can discern are sand, gravel, and ripgut.

As I study the dirt, I notice that cars passing on Sandpiper are slowing down. In each a lone man is driving, and every one of these guys seems to stare at me as he cruises by. I remember that this isolated street is reputedly a gay pick-up area. Are these drivers looking for a good time, or are they staring at my socks, still pulled up over the cuffs of my pants? I swing around and tramp back toward the wilds, where I know what I'm getting into and no one cares if I'm committing a fashion felony.

I descend the back side of the dunes onto twenty-four acres of grasslands—a degraded remnant of the Los Angeles coastal prairie. Tucked between the dunes and the airport, the flat meadow I see today bears little resemblance to its ancient predecessor. The real thing is extinct; all nine hundred square miles are gone. Excavated, replanted, paved. Vast seas of shimmering bunchgrass have been plowed under. The vernal pools, choked with wildflowers in late spring, have vanished, replaced by today's dominant form of life on the coastal prairie—the apartment dweller.

On this little fragment of pseudo-prairie, ripgut is now the dominant plant. But that's not necessarily a reason to despair. In fact, it's an improvement. Just a few years ago this field was dominated by California buckwheat, the bane of the El Segundo blue butterfly. AgResearch, in one of their first efforts to boost the butterfly population, cleared the California buckwheat and reintroduced the dune species. Now dune buckwheat is spreading across the meadow, and the blue butterfly's numbers are rebounding. A census in 1990 counted 3,500 adults, almost a tenfold increase. Rudi Mattoni thinks the population could soon exceed 10,000. And lately there have been other signs of success. The San Diego horned lizard has been spotted all over the preserve. Several pairs of kestrels have recently settled in the dunes. A burrowing owl, not seen near the dunes for years, chose to nest on the prairie this spring.

Despite these successes, Rudi Mattoni is not enthusiastic about his efforts to reconstruct an extinct ecology such as the coastal prairie. "When people talk about grassland reconstruction," he scoffs, "they don't know what they're talking about. There's no prescription. We don't know what to do. How do you learn to walk?"

His first wobbling step was to eliminate the California buckwheat. For the most part that has worked. Now he is trying to drive out the nonnative grasses by reintroducing the native *Stipa cernua,* a bunchgrass. If the *Stipa* does indeed beat back the European grasses, Mattoni's next toddling step looks more difficult. He believes these fields were probably dominated by annual plants. How to choose, find, and distribute those seeds, Mattoni shrugs, "is anybody's guess."

On a misty day last December, working with a team of giggly teenagers, I planted sprigs of *Stipa*—shoots of grass not more than a few inches tall. Today I walk the edge of the meadow, inspecting our handiwork. Those sprigs have grown into thick tufts three feet tall. Waving in the wind, their feathery seed tops look like corn silk. When I see the fruits of our labor—or in this case, the grains—I swell with a sense of accomplishment. I suppose this is the same pride farmers have known at harvest time for millennia, but for me it's a new sensation. It makes me want to till my own forty acres.

Several years ago Rudi Mattoni found this *Stipa* growing, miraculously, on a little plot of airport land that was about to be bulldozed. He rescued two hundred bunches and replanted them in a corner of this meadow. The transplants took, and now shimmering *Stipa* is crowding out the ripgut.

I exhort the American grasses to succeed in their counterattack on the European invaders. "Oh God of battles! Steel my soldiers' hearts; possess them not with fear." As I review the valiant American bunchgrass troops, I feel a stabbing pain in my ankle.

Scorpion!

I look down. It's just a foxtail impaling my foot. (A covert operation by those sneaky European grasses.) Time for a sock cleanout.

I sit in the sand at the edge of the back dune. Beside me grows a plant named *Haplopappus ericoides,* or goldenbush. It is a dense, dark-green shrub that lives to be forty or fifty years old. In autumn the bush explodes with golden blossoms; its petals grow so thick they obscure the plant's leaves. Although goldenbush can sometimes be raised from cuttings, it usually resists human efforts at propagation. Its seeds are viable for only a short time in autumn, and they seem to require a specific combination of conditions to germinate.

Good intentions are not always enough when humans attempt to steer the development of a natural system. Plenty of knowledge is necessary, knowledge we humans have usually not yet earned. Like the complex relationship between the El Segundo blue butterfly and two species of buckwheat, forces that we do not fully understand may control the spread of *Haplopappus*.

The sheer complexity of an ecosystem is staggering. Rudi Mattoni has spent years in this relatively simple dune community trying to understand the interplay between a few species. Approximately sixty other species of flora and fauna inhabit the El Segundo dunes, not to mention untold microscopic creatures. Imagine how many other lives are laced together here in the web of life. Imagine the web that enshrouds the globe. If every human on earth spent several years researching and writing a dissertation on a single biological relationship, we still would not begin to understand how the world's ecological systems work—not that anyone could sew all those scraps of knowledge into one coherent quilt.

I look to the venerable old shrub beside me to see if it can impart some wisdom on the subject. But the *Haplopappus* offers no Delphic pronouncements. If we humans want to understand the natural world, I suppose we must stumble ahead the old-fashioned way—one dissertation at a time.

As I sit, a kestrel swoops across the meadow, then flaps its wings to hover above a single spot, studying some creature below. Kestrels are often called sparrowhawks, but sometimes they are also known as hoverhawks because of this unusual ability to hang suspended in the air. Just then a Korean Air Lines 747 thunders toward us. The kestrel stops hovering and flees for its life.

Unfortunately, I have no such escape. The monstrous airliner flies so low, its massive engines shake the diaphragm muscles in my chest, making me cough.

I resist the urge to fire a shoulder-launched missile at the 747. Instead I grudgingly acknowledge that this plane is the reason the meadow before me now grows buckwheat and not

Taco Bells. Still, if larger vertebrates are ever going to successfully re-establish themselves in the wash of these airplanes, I
fear the poor creatures will be deaf. Or psychotic.

•

I climb the steep back face of the dune and bear south on the
last leg of my circumnavigation. The area I am passing has received the most attention from Rhapsody in Green over the
last four years. The plantlife here looks almost as rich as those
parts of the dunes that were never disturbed. Although ripgut
and storksbill still grow in some stretches, so do all kinds of
natives. Primrose, deerweed, bush sunflower, dove lupine,
bush lupine, sun cups, telegraph weed, bladderpod. The latter had been extirpated from the dunes, but AgResearch reintroduced them, and now they grow in many places. Dune
buckwheat plants in their third and fourth generation are
flourishing. Rudi Mattoni declares, "It looks the way dunes
are supposed to look."

The most successful volunteer effort on the dunes is called
Adopt-an-Acre. Volunteers who show up several times are
offered a plot of land for which they can take responsibility.
They tend their acre by weeding out alien species and planting natives. Their goal is to create a garden that flourishes—
until one year it blows away in a strong wind, as a healthy
dune should.

About the Adopt-an-Acre program Jon Earl says, "There's
something wonderful for the soul to have a small task, a small
piece of property to maintain. There's a finite number of
things to do, and if you get them done you feel relaxed and
refreshed."

Walking along these adopted acres, I see that one foster
parent has delimited his plot with a wall of broken concrete,
a tiny corollary to a Yankee stone wall. Another acre is com-

pletely free of brome. On hands and knees this volunteer painstakingly eradicated every last shoot of alien grass.

Ellen Petty adds, "The Adopt-an-Acre people learn about everything. They see the [natural] interactions. When something blooms in their area they get very excited. They share it with the people around them. They get to know their neighbors. People start talking to people. Everybody works together. If someone is absent one week, people work in that person's plot."

So here in the middle of Los Angeles every third Sunday people are showing up with a regularity that many church congregations would envy, and these people are tithing with their sweat to rebuild a natural habitat. While they are restoring homes for horned lizards, kestrels, and butterflies, they are also building something else that is almost extinct in a city like Los Angeles—a sense of community.

•

Despite the many successes AgResearch and Rhapsody in Green have fashioned at the El Segundo dunes, the long-term forecast for this preserve looks cloudy. Rudi Mattoni feels it requires little more human intervention. Ideally the roads should be torn out, but that's not vital. A few more acres must be cleared of iceplant and acacia. Mostly the land just needs to be monitored, since iceplant will keep sprouting for years, and acacia trees could pop up for decades.

To recreate the dunes' original ecology, larger vertebrates, such as rabbits, weasels, and several species of snakes, should be introduced. A resident population of European red foxes makes that difficult. They devour almost all forms of live meat, excluding humans, that set foot on the dunes. Adriano Mattoni has made some efforts to relocate them but has been thwarted by the "humaniacs," as he calls them—the animal rights advocates more concerned with the techniques used to relocate foxes than with the rare birds and reptiles being torn to shreds by the red fox, a creature that by all rights should be romping around merry old England and not El Segundo.

These lingering environmental problems, however, are probably no longer the biggest dangers to the dunes. Today the worst threats are political.

Rudi Mattoni's grants are expiring, and his sometimes prickly personality has annoyed enough people in both the city and airport bureaucracies that he and AgResearch will probably not be granted more money to continue their work at the dunes. Any future duties Rudi Mattoni performs here will be as a volunteer.

Where the money would come from to maintain the dunes is unclear. Mattoni estimates that there's enough work for a full-time restorationist and some continuing volunteer efforts, particularly the Adopt-an-Acre program. In June 1994 a statewide ballot proposition to support parklands earmarked millions of dollars for the El Segundo dunes. But California voters demonstrated a sense of fiscal prudence not shared in recent years by their elected officials. They voted the proposition down, along with every other bond measure appearing on the ballot.

Several concerned organizations like the Los Angeles chapter of the Audubon Society are proposing the formation of a nonprofit Los Angeles Dunes Conservancy. Their hope is to depoliticize the dunes by giving representation to the various parties interested in the fate of the preserve. This board could oversee the actions of the city agency entrusted with administering the dunes, as well as any other human intervention occurring there.

At this time it's all up in the air. Without a little funding, all work will soon stop, even the volunteer efforts. The city's agreement with the Coastal Commission obligates them to maintain two hundred acres as a wild preserve, but Los Angeles, like a lot of California municipalities in the mid-1990s, is virtually broke. Many voices clamor for any funds the city can spare. For a bare-bones maintenance program, Los Angeles must allocate only about $50,000 a year, but without at least that much money the city stands to lose this remarkable natural treasure, to say nothing of the million dollars already spent here and the sweat of thousands of volunteers.

•

I stop at one of the highest points on the dunes, a site volunteers recently cleared of invasive vegetation. Huge heaps of iceplant, still bright green with life, bulge up all over the site. The feet of those well-meaning volunteers have trampled almost every square foot of the block—a necessary evil when you're pulling weeds.

From this vantage point I can see the airport and beyond that the great grid of the city stretching to the east until it disappears into the smog. To the west sweeps the vast blue arc of Santa Monica Bay. The sun has finally burned through the overcast, and it sparkles on the waves.

Looking up and down the ridge, I dream the land once more.

First, I see acacia trees springing up from the sand, locking arms, and goosestepping across the hills. Tendrils of iceplant snake out from the haystacks of rotting plants that litter the preserve. Green shoots fan out and weave together. In a heartbeat they swallow the El Segundo dunes in one giant photosynthetic gulp.

Then I dream the land another way.

In this vision the iceplant and acacia are gone. The sand hills blaze with riots of wildflowers. Flocks of quail cluck and dart through the underbrush. Above the beach, least terns wheel in the breeze. Sand shifts endlessly before the Pacific winds. Lizards scramble across the ruins left behind by giants who once walked this land.

Ubi sunt?

This race was not driven from their homes by barbarians. No, these people had the grace to give their land willingly back to its original inhabitants. For these giants the wisest use of the land was to make it wild.

As I dream, my eyes fix on a plant growing in the trampled sand just six inches from the sidewalk. This small green bush is not another figment of my imagination; it's real. I stoop to inspect and see it's a goldenbush—the plant we lordly humans have such difficulty cultivating. On its own, far from its brothers on the back dune, this bush has laid claim to the crest of the hill.

Why?

Scientists could doubtless provide a well-reasoned hypothesis, but I prefer to see this young goldenbush as a ray of hope, a dream becoming reality. Here is confirmation that the El Segundo dunes are regaining some of the natural rhythms they lost long ago. In an era of ozone holes, toxic stews, global warming, drug-resistant bacteria, and countless other symptoms of an impending environmental Armageddon, a single plant growing in the shadow of LAX marks a path that could lead us away from the brink. The little goldenbush points to a time and place where mankind and Nature can live as one.

I see the land awakening from a long, fitful slumber.